How to

Prepare & Can

Vegetables

& More

Preserving Nature's Bounty

 Publications International, Ltd.

The home-canning content in this publication was adapted from the U.S. Department of Agriculture's Agricultural Information Bulletin Number 539, *Complete Guide to Home Canning,* which was reprinted with revisions in June 2006.

The brand-name products mentioned in this publication are trademarks or service marks of their respective companies. The mention of any product in this publication does not constitute an endorsement by the respective proprietors of Publications International, Ltd., nor does it constitute an endorsement by any of these companies that their products should be used in the manner recommended by this publication.

The publishers would like to thank the following organizations for the use of their recipes in the BONUS section of this publication: National Turkey Federation and The Sugar Association, Inc.

Picture Credits:
Cover: Gim Lenora/Getty Images
Interior Illustration: Thinkstock Photos

Louis Weber, CEO
Publications International, Ltd.
7373 North Cicero Avenue
Lincolnwood, Illinois 60712

Permission is never granted for commercial purposes.

ISBN-13: 978-1-4508-0644-2
ISBN-10: 1-4508-0644-9

Manufactured in USA.

8 7 6 5 4 3 2 1

Caution: All home-canned foods should be canned according to the procedures in this guide. Low-acid and tomato foods not canned according to the recommendations in this publication or according to other USDA-endorsed recommendations present a risk of botulism. If it is possible that any deviation from the USDA-endorsed methods occurred, to prevent the risk of botulism, low-acid and tomato foods should be boiled in a saucepan before being consumed even if you detect no signs of spoilage. At altitudes below 1,000 feet, boil foods for 10 minutes. Add an additional minute of boiling time for each additional 1,000 feet of elevation. However, this is not intended to serve as a recommendation for consuming foods known to be significantly underprocessed according to current standards and recommended methods. It is not a guarantee that all possible defects and hazards with nonrecommended methods can be overcome by this boiling process. The recommendation is to only can low-acid and tomato foods according to the procedures in this guide.

Reference to commercial products and services is made with the understanding that no discrimination is intended and no endorsement by the U. S. Department of Agriculture is implied. Clear Jel® and Splenda® are mentioned because they are the only suitable products presently available to the general public for the stated purposes in given products.

Research is continually being conducted in areas that affect food preservation recommendations. Make sure your food preservation information is always current, with up-to-date, tested guidelines.

For Safety's Sake

Pressure canning is the only recommended method for canning meat, poultry, seafood, and vegetables. The bacterium *Clostridium botulinum* is destroyed in low-acid foods when they are processed at the correct time and pressure in pressure canners. Using boiling-water canners for these foods poses a real risk of botulism poisoning.

If *Clostridium botulinum* bacteria survive and grow inside a sealed jar of food, they can produce a poisonous toxin. Even a taste of food containing this toxin can be fatal. Boiling food 10 minutes at altitudes below 1,000 feet should destroy this poison when it is present. For altitudes at and above 1,000 feet, add 1 additional minute per 1,000 feet additional elevation.

Caution: To prevent the risk of botulism, low-acid and tomato foods not canned according to the recommendations in this publication or according to other USDA-endorsed recommendations should be boiled, as above, in a saucepan before consuming, even if you detect no signs of spoilage. This is not intended to serve as a recommendation for consuming foods known to be significantly underprocessed according to current standards and recommended methods. It is not a guarantee that all possible defects and hazards with other methods can be overcome by this boiling process. All low-acid foods canned according to the approved recommendations may be eaten without boiling them when you are sure of all the following:

⬥ Food was processed in a pressure canner.

⬥ Gauge of the pressure canner was accurate.

⬥ Up-to-date, researched process times and pressures were used for the size of jar, style of pack, and kind of food being canned.

⬥ The process time and pressure recommended for sterilizing the food at your altitude were followed.

⬥ Jar lid is firmly sealed and concave.

⬥ Nothing has leaked from jar.

⬥ No liquid spurts out when jar is opened.

⬥ No unnatural or "off" odors can be detected.

Do Your Canned Foods Pass This Test?

Overall appearance

⬥ Good proportion of solid to liquid

⬥ Full pack with proper headspace

⬥ Liquid just covering solid

⬥ Free of air bubbles

⬥ Free of imperfections—stems, cores, seeds

⬥ Good seals

⬥ Practical pack that is done quickly and easily

Fruit and vegetables

❖ Pieces uniform in size and shape

❖ Characteristic, uniform color

❖ Shape retained—not broken or mushy

❖ Proper maturity

Liquid or syrup

❖ Clear and free from sediment

Determining Your Altitude Above Sea Level

It is important to know your approximate elevation, or altitude above sea level, in order to determine a safe processing time for canned foods. Since the boiling temperature of liquid is lower at higher elevations, it is critical that additional time be given for the safe processing of foods at altitudes above sea level.

It is not practical to include a list of altitudes in this guide, since there is wide variation within a state and even a county. For example, the state of Kansas has areas with altitudes varying between 75 feet and 4,039 feet above sea level. Kansas is not generally thought to have high altitudes, but there are many areas of the state where adjustments for altitude must be considered. Colorado, on the other hand, has people living in areas between 3,000 feet and 10,000 feet above sea level. They tend to be more conscious of the need to make altitude adjustments in the various processing schedules. To list altitudes for specific counties may actually be misleading, due to the differences in geographic terrain within a county.

If you are unsure about the altitude where you will be canning foods, consult your county Cooperative Extension agent. An alternative source of information would be your local district conservationist with the Soil Conservation Service.

Contents

⋄ ⌃ ⋄ ⌃

❖ ◈ ❖ ◈

Chapter 3: Preparing and Canning Fermented Foods and Pickled Vegetables. 83

Fermented Foods 87

Cucumber Pickles 91

❖ ◇ ❖ ◇

❖ ◇ ❖ ◇

Chapter 1

Principles of Home Canning

Why can foods?

CANNING CAN BE a safe and economical way to preserve quality food at home. Disregarding the value of your labor, canning homegrown food may save you half the cost of buying commercially canned food. Canning favorite and special products to be enjoyed by family and friends is a fulfilling experience and a source of pride for many people.

Many vegetables begin losing some of their vitamins when harvested. Nearly half the vitamins may be lost within a few days unless the fresh produce is refrigerated or preserved. Within 1 to 2 weeks, even refrigerated produce loses half or more of some of its vitamins. The heating process during canning destroys from a third to half of vitamins A and C, thiamin, and riboflavin. Once the produce is canned, additional losses of these sensitive vitamins are from 5 to 20 percent each year. The amounts of other vitamins, however, are only slightly lower in canned compared with fresh produce. If vegetables are handled properly and canned promptly after harvest, they can be more nutritious than fresh produce sold in local stores.

The advantages of home canning are lost, however, when you start with poor-quality fresh foods; when jars fail to seal properly; when food spoils; and when flavors, texture, color, and nutrients deteriorate during prolonged storage.

The information that follows explains many of these problems and recommends ways to minimize them.

How canning preserves foods

The high percentage of water in most fresh foods makes them very perishable. They spoil or lose their quality for several reasons:

- growth of undesirable microorganisms—bacteria, molds, and yeasts;
- activity of food enzymes;
- reactions with oxygen;
- moisture loss.

Microorganisms live and multiply quickly on the surfaces of fresh food and on the inside of bruised, insect-damaged, and diseased food. Oxygen and enzymes are present throughout the insides of fresh foods.

Proper canning practices include:

❖ carefully selecting and washing fresh food,
❖ peeling some fresh foods,
❖ hot-packing many foods (see pages 21–22),
❖ adding acids (lemon juice or vinegar) to some foods,
❖ using acceptable jars and self-sealing lids,
❖ processing jars in a boiling-water or pressure canner for the correct period of time.

Collectively, these practices remove oxygen; destroy enzymes; prevent the growth of undesirable bacteria, yeasts, and molds; and help form a high vacuum in jars. A high vacuum is good because it forms a tight seal that keeps liquid in and air and microorganisms out.

Ensuring safe canned foods

Growth of the bacterium *Clostridium botulinum* in canned food may cause botulism—a deadly form of food poisoning. These bacteria exist either as spores or as vegetative cells. The spores, which are comparable to plant seeds, can survive harmlessly in soil and water for many years. When ideal conditions exist for growth, the spores produce vegetative cells, which multiply rapidly and may produce a deadly toxin within 3 to 4 days of growth in an environment consisting of:

✤ a moist, low-acid food;
✤ a temperature between 40° and 120°F;
✤ less than 2 percent oxygen.

Botulinum spores are on the outer surfaces of most fresh foods. Because they grow only in the absence of air, they are harmless on the exterior of these foods.

Most bacteria, yeasts, and molds are difficult to remove from food surfaces. Washing fresh food reduces their numbers only slightly. Peeling root crops, underground-stem crops, and tomatoes reduces their numbers greatly. Blanching also helps. But the vital controls are using the appropriate method of canning and making sure the recommended research-based process times, found in this guide, are used.

The processing times in this guide ensure destruction of the largest expected number of heat-resistant microorganisms in home-canned foods. Properly sterilized canned food will be free of spoilage if lids seal and jars are stored below 95°F. Storing jars at 50° to 70°F enhances retention of quality.

Food acidity and processing methods
Whether food should be processed in a pressure canner or boiling-water canner to control botulinum bacteria depends

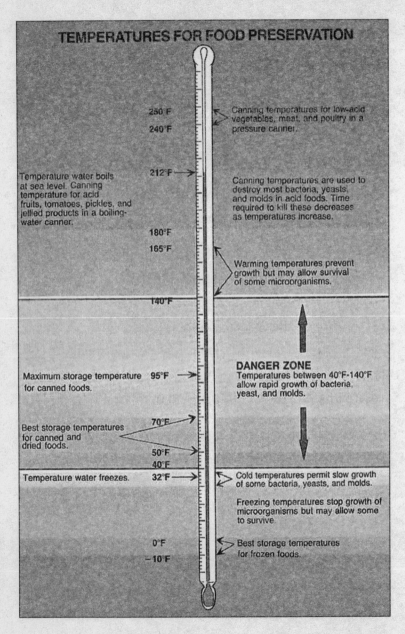

TEMPERATURES FOR FOOD PRESERVATION

250°F
240°F

Canning temperatures for low-acid vegetables, meat, and poultry in a pressure canner.

212°F

Temperature water boils at sea level. Canning temperature for acid fruits, tomatoes, pickles, and jellied products in a boiling-water canner.

Canning temperatures are used to destroy most bacteria, yeasts, and molds in acid foods. Time required to kill these decreases as temperatures increase.

180°F
165°F

Warming temperatures prevent growth but may allow survival of some microorganisms.

140°F

DANGER ZONE
Temperatures between 40°F-140°F allow rapid growth of bacteria, yeast, and molds.

95°F

Maximum storage temperature for canned foods.

70°F

Best storage temperatures for canned and dried foods.

50°F
40°F
32°F

Temperature water freezes.

Cold temperatures permit slow growth of some bacteria, yeasts, and molds.

Freezing temperatures stop growth of microorganisms but may allow some to survive.

0°F
−10°F

Best storage temperatures for frozen foods.

on the acidity of the food. Acidity may be natural, as in most fruits, or added, as in pickled food. *Low-acid* canned foods are not acidic enough to prevent the growth of these bacteria. *Acid* foods contain enough acid to block their growth or destroy them more rapidly when heated. The term "pH" is a measure of acidity; the lower its value, the more acid the food. The acidity level in foods can be increased by adding lemon juice, citric acid, or vinegar.

Low-acid foods have pH values higher than 4.6. They include red meats, seafood, poultry, milk, and all fresh vegetables except for most tomatoes. Most mixtures of low-acid and acid foods also have pH values above 4.6 unless their recipes include enough lemon juice, citric acid, or vinegar to make them acid foods. Acid foods have a pH of 4.6 or lower. They include fruits, pickles, sauerkraut, jams, jellies, marmalades, and fruit butters.

Although tomatoes usually are considered an acid food, some are now known to have pH values slightly above 4.6. Figs also have pH values slightly above 4.6. Therefore, if they are to be canned as acid foods, these products must be acidified to a pH of 4.6 or lower with lemon juice or citric acid. Properly acidified tomatoes and figs are acid foods and can be safely processed in a boiling-water canner.

Botulinum spores are very hard to destroy at boiling-water temperatures; the higher the canner temperature, the more easily they are destroyed. Therefore, all low-acid foods should be sterilized at temperatures of 240° to 250°F, attainable with pressure canners operated at 10 to 15 PSIG. PSIG means pounds per square inch of pressure as measured by gauge. The more familiar "PSI" designation is used hereafter in this publication. At temperatures of 240° to 250°F, the time needed to destroy bacteria in low-acid canned food ranges from 20 to 100 minutes. The exact time depends on the kind of food being canned, the way it is packed into jars, and the size of the jars. The time needed to safely process low-acid foods in a boiling-water canner ranges from 7 to 11 hours; the time needed to process acid foods in boiling water varies from 5 to 85 minutes.

Process adjustments at high altitudes

Using the process time for canning food at sea level may result in spoilage if you live at altitudes of 1,000 feet or more. That's because water boils at lower temperatures as altitude increases. Lower boiling temperatures are less effective for killing bacteria. Increasing the process time or canner pressure compensates for lower boiling temperatures. Therefore, when you use the canning recipes in this guide, select the proper processing time or canner pressure for the

altitude where you live. If you do not know the altitude, contact your local county Cooperative Extension agent. An alternative source of information would be the local district conservationist with the Soil Conservation Service.

Equipment and methods not recommended

Open-kettle canning and the processing of freshly filled jars in conventional ovens, microwave ovens, and dishwashers are not recommended, because these practices do not prevent all risks of spoilage. Steam canners are not recommended because processing times for use with current models have not been adequately researched. Because steam canners do not heat foods in the same manner as boiling-water canners, their use with boiling-water process times may result in spoilage. It is not recommended that pressure processes in excess of 15 PSI be applied when using new pressure-canning equipment. So-called canning powders are useless as preservatives and do not replace the need for proper heat processing. Jars with wire bails and glass caps make attractive antiques or storage containers for dry food ingredients but are not recommended for use in canning. One-piece zinc porcelain-lined caps are also no longer recommended. Both glass and zinc caps use flat rubber rings for sealing jars but too often fail to seal properly.

Ensuring high-quality canned foods

Begin with good-quality fresh foods suitable for canning. Quality varies among varieties of fruits and vegetables. Many county Cooperative Extension offices can recommend varieties best suited for canning. Examine food carefully for freshness and wholesomeness. Discard diseased and moldy food. Trim small diseased lesions or spots from food.

Can fruits and vegetables picked from your garden or purchased from nearby growers when the products are at their peak of quality—within 6 to 12 hours after harvest for most vegetables. For best quality, apricots, nectarines, peaches, pears, and plums should be ripened 1 or more days between harvest and canning. If you must delay the canning of other fresh produce, keep it in a shady, cool place.

Maintaining color and flavor in canned food

To maintain good natural color and flavor in stored canned food, you must:

◆ Remove oxygen from food tissues and jars.
◆ Quickly destroy the food enzymes.
◆ Obtain high jar vacuums and airtight jar seals.

Follow these guidelines to ensure that your canned foods retain their optimum colors and flavors during both processing and storage:

◆ Use only high-quality foods that are at the proper maturity and are free of diseases and bruises.
◆ Use the hot-pack method, especially with acid foods to be processed in boiling water.
◆ Don't unnecessarily expose prepared foods to air. Can them as soon as possible.
◆ While preparing a canner load of jars, keep peeled, halved, quartered, sliced, or diced apples, apricots, nectarines, peaches, and pears in a solution of 3 grams (3,000 milligrams) ascorbic acid to 1 gallon of cold water. This procedure is also useful in maintaining the natural color of mushrooms and potatoes and for preventing

stem-end discoloration in cherries and grapes. You can get ascorbic acid in several forms:

PURE POWDERED FORM—seasonally available among canners' supplies in supermarkets. One level teaspoon of pure powder weighs about 3 grams. Use 1 teaspoon per gallon water.

VITAMIN C TABLETS—economical and available year-round in many stores. Buy 500 milligram tablets; crush and dissolve 6 tablets per gallon water.

COMMERCIALLY PREPARED MIXES OF ASCORBIC AND CITRIC ACID—seasonally available among canners' supplies in supermarkets. Citric-acid powder alone may be sold in supermarkets, but it is less effective in controlling discoloration. If you use these products, follow the manufacturer's directions.

- ❖ Fill jars with hot foods, and adjust headspace as specified in recipes.
- ❖ Tighten screw bands securely, but if you are especially strong, not as tightly as possible.
- ❖ Process and cool jars.
- ❖ Store the jars in a relatively cool, dark place, preferably between 50° and 70°F.
- ❖ Can no more food than you will use within a year.

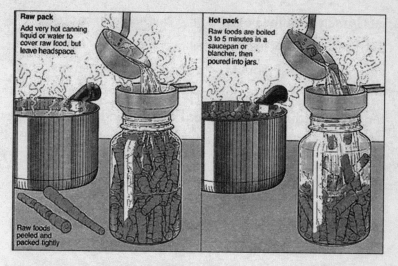

Raw pack
Add very hot canning liquid or water to cover raw food, but leave headspace.

Hot pack
Raw foods are boiled 3 to 5 minutes in a saucepan or blancher, then poured into jars.

Raw foods peeled and packed tightly

Advantages of hot-packing

Many fresh foods contain from 10 to more than 30 percent air. How long canned foods retain their high quality depends on how much air is removed from the food before the jars are sealed.

Raw-packing is the practice of filling jars tightly with freshly prepared but unheated food. Such foods, especially fruit, will float in the jars. The entrapped air in and around the food may cause discoloration within 2 to 3 months of storage. Raw-packing is more suitable for vegetables processed in a pressure canner.

Hot-packing is the practice of heating freshly prepared food to boiling, simmering it 2 to 5 minutes, and promptly filling jars loosely with the boiled food. Whether food has been hot-packed or raw-packed, the juice, syrup, or water to be added to the foods should be heated to boiling before being added to the jars. This practice helps to remove air from food tissues, shrinks food, helps keep the food from floating in the jars, increases vacuum in sealed jars, and improves shelf life. Preshrinking food allows more food to fit into each jar.

Hot-packing is the best way to remove air and is the preferred pack style for foods processed in a boiling-water canner. At first, the color of hot-packed foods may appear no better than that of raw-packed foods, but within a short storage period, both color and flavor of hot-packed foods will be superior.

Controlling headspace

The unfilled space above the food in a jar and below its lid is termed headspace. Directions for canning specify leaving ¼ inch for jams and jellies, ½ inch for fruits and tomatoes to be processed in boiling water, and from 1 to 1¼ inches for low-acid foods to be processed in a pressure canner. This space is needed for expansion of food as jars are processed and for forming vacuums in cooled jars. The extent of expansion is determined by the air content in the food and by the processing temperature. Air expands greatly when heated to high

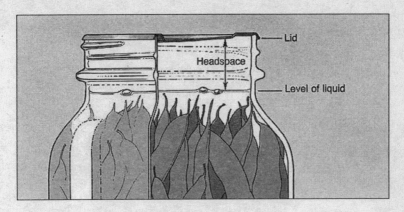

temperatures; the higher the temperature, the greater the expansion. Foods expand less than air does when heated.

Jars and lids

Food may be canned in glass jars or metal containers. Metal containers can be used only once. They require special sealing equipment and are much more costly than jars.

Regular and wide-mouth Mason-type, threaded, home-canning jars with self-sealing lids are the best choice. They are available in half-pint, pint, 1½-pint, quart, and half-gallon sizes. The mouth opening of a standard jar is about 2⅜ inches. Wide-mouth jars have openings of about 3 inches, making them more easily filled and emptied. Half-gallon jars may be used for canning very acid juices. Regular-mouth decorator jelly jars are available in 8- and

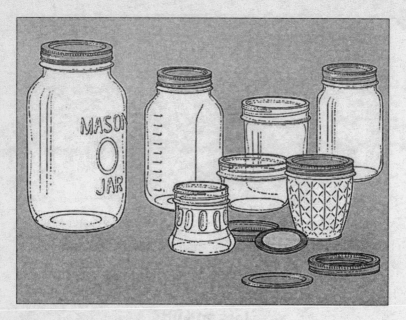

12-ounce sizes. With careful use and handling, Mason jars may be reused many times, requiring only new lids each time. When jars and lids are used properly, jar seals and vacuums are excellent and jar breakage is rare.

Most commercial pint- and quart-size mayonnaise or salad-dressing jars may be used with new two-piece lids for canning acid foods. However, you should expect more seal failures and jar breakage. These jars have a narrower sealing surface and are tempered less than Mason jars and may be weakened by repeated contact with metal spoons or knives used in dispensing mayonnaise or salad dressing. Seemingly insignificant scratches in glass may cause cracking and breakage while the jars are being processed in a canner. Mayonnaise-type jars are not recommended for use with foods to be processed in a pressure canner because of excessive jar breakage. Other commercial jars with mouths that cannot be sealed with two-piece canning lids are not recommended for use in canning any food at home.

Jar cleaning and preparation

Before every use, wash empty jars in hot water with detergent and rinse well by hand, or wash in a dishwasher. Unrinsed detergent residues may cause unnatural flavors and colors. Jars should be kept hot until ready to fill with food. In a large stockpot or boiling-water canner, submerge the clean, empty jars in enough water to cover them. Bring the water to a simmer (180°F) and keep the jars in the simmering water until it is time to fill them with food. A dishwasher may be used for preheating jars if they are washed and dried on a complete regular cycle. Keep the jars in the closed dishwasher until needed for filling.

These washing and preheating methods do not sterilize jars. Some used jars may have a white film on the exterior surface caused by mineral deposits. This scale, or hard-water film, on jars is easily removed by soaking jars several hours in a solution containing 1 cup of vinegar (5 percent acidity) per gallon of water prior to washing and preheating the jars.

Sterilization of empty jars

All jams, jellies, and pickled products that will be processed less than 10 minutes should go into sterile empty jars. To sterilize empty jars after washing in detergent and rinsing thoroughly, submerge them, right side up, in a boiling-water canner with the rack in the bottom. Fill the canner with warm water to 1 inch above the jar tops. Bring the water to a boil, and boil 10 minutes at altitudes of less than 1,000 feet. At higher elevations, boil 1 additional minute for each additional 1,000 feet elevation. Reduce the heat under the canner, and keep the jars in the hot water until it is time to fill them. Remove and drain hot sterilized jars one at a time, saving the hot water in the canner for processing filled jars. Fill the sterilized jars with food, add lids, and tighten screw bands.

Empty jars that will be filled with vegetables or fruits and processed in a pressure canner need not be presterilized. It is also unnecessary to presterilize jars for fruits, tomatoes, and pickled or fermented foods that will be processed 10 minutes or longer in a boiling-water canner.

Lid selection, preparation, and use

The common self-sealing lid consists of a flat metal lid held in place during processing by a metal screw band. The flat lid is crimped around its bottom edge to form a trough, which is filled with a colored gasket compound. When jars

Metal screw band

Metal lid

Jar

Sealing compound

are processed, the lid gasket softens and flows slightly to cover the jar-sealing surface yet allows air to escape from the jar. The gasket then forms an airtight seal as the jar cools. Gaskets in unused lids work well for at least 5 years from date of manufacture. The gasket compound in older unused lids may fail to seal on jars.

Buy only the quantity of lids you will use in a year. To ensure a good seal, carefully follow the manufacturer's directions in preparing lids for use. Examine all metal lids carefully. Do not use old, dented, or deformed lids or lids with gaps or other defects in the sealing gasket.

When directions say to fill jars and adjust lids, use the following procedures: After filling jars with food and adding covering liquid, release air bubbles by inserting a flat plastic (not metal) spatula between the food and the jar. Slowly turn the jar and move the spatula up and down to allow air bubbles to escape. (It is not necessary to release air bubbles from jars of jams, jellies, or all-liquid foods such as juices.) Adjust the headspace and then clean the jar rim (sealing surface) with a dampened paper towel. Place the preheated lid, gasket down,

1. Add salt, if desired.

2. Remove air bubbles with plastic utensil.

3. Wipe upper rim of jar completely for a good seal.

4. Assemble lid.

Metal screw band

Sealing compound under metal lid

5. Remove screw band for reuse after processing, once jar has cooled.

onto the cleaned jar-sealing surface. (Uncleaned jar-sealing surfaces may cause seal failures.) Then fit the metal screw band over the flat lid. Follow the lid-manufacturer's guidelines enclosed with or on the box for tightening the jar lids properly.

Do not retighten lids after processing jars. As jars cool, the contents in the jar contract, pulling the self-sealing lid firmly against the jar to form a high vacuum.

◆ If lids are too loose, liquid may escape from jars during processing, and seals may fail.

◆ If lids are too tight, air cannot vent during processing, and food will discolor during storage. Overtightening also may cause lids to buckle and jars to break, especially with raw-packed, pressure-processed food.

Screw bands are not needed on stored jars. They can be removed easily after jars have cooled. When removed, washed, dried, and stored in a dry area, screw bands may be used many times. If left on stored jars, they become difficult to remove, often rust, and may not work properly again.

Recommended canners

Equipment for heat-processing home-canned food is of 2 main types—boiling-water canners and pressure canners. Most are designed to hold 7 quart jars or 8 to 9 pints. Small pressure canners hold 4 quart jars; some large pressure canners hold 18 pint jars in 2 layers but hold only 7 quart jars. Pressure saucepans with smaller capacities are not recommended for canning. Small-capacity pressure canners are treated much like standard larger canners and should be vented using the typical venting procedures.

Low-acid foods must be processed in a pressure canner to be free of botulism risks. Although pressure canners may also be used for processing acid foods, boiling-water canners are recommended for this purpose because they are faster. A pressure canner would require from 55 to 100 minutes to process a load of jars, while the total time for processing most acid foods in boiling water varies from 25 to 60 minutes. A boiling-water canner loaded with filled jars requires about 20 to 30 minutes of heating before its water begins to boil. A loaded pressure canner requires about 12 to 15 minutes of heating before it begins to vent; another 10 minutes to vent the canner; another 5 minutes to pressurize the canner; another 8 to 10 minutes to process the acid food; and, finally, another 20 to 60 minutes to cool the canner before removing jars.

Boiling-water canners

These canners are made of aluminum or porcelain-covered steel. They have removable, perforated racks and fitted lids.

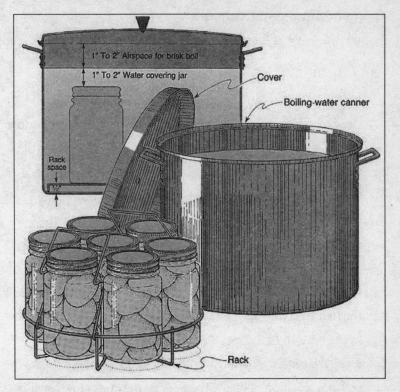

The canner must be deep enough to accommodate at least 1 inch of briskly boiling water over the tops of the jars during processing. Some boiling-water canners do not have flat bottoms. However, a canner with a flat bottom must be used on an electric range. Either a flat or ridged bottom can be used on a gas burner. To ensure uniform processing of all jars when an electric range is being used, the canner should be no more than 4 inches wider in diameter than the element on which it is heated.

Using boiling-water canners

Follow these steps for successful boiling-water canning:

1. Before you start preparing your food, fill the canner halfway with clean water. This is approximately the level needed for a canner load of pint jars. For other sizes and numbers of jars, the amount of water in the canner will need to be adjusted so it will be 1 to 2 inches over the top of the filled jars.

2. Preheat water to 140°F for raw-packed foods and to 180°F for hot-packed foods. Food preparation can begin while this water is preheating.

3. Load filled jars, fitted with lids, into the canner rack, and use the handles to lower the rack into the water; or put the rack in the bottom of the canner and fill it, one jar at a time, using a jar lifter. When using a jar lifter, make sure it is securely positioned below the neck of the jar (below the lid's screw band). Keep the jar upright at all times. Tilting the jar could cause food to spill into the sealing area of the lid.

4. Add more boiling water, if needed, so the water level is at least 1 inch above the jar tops. For process times over 30 minutes, the water level should be at least 2 inches above the tops of the jars.

5. Turn heat to its highest position, cover the canner with its lid, and heat until the water in the canner boils vigorously.

6. Set a timer for the total minutes required for processing the food.

7. Keep the canner covered and maintain a boil throughout the process schedule. The heat setting may be lowered a little as long as a complete boil is maintained for the entire process time. If the water stops boiling at any time during the process, bring the water back to a vigorous boil and begin the timing of the process over, from the beginning.

8. Add more boiling water, if needed, to keep the water level above the jars.

9. When jars have been boiled for the recommended time, turn off the heat and remove the canner lid. Wait 5 minutes before removing jars.

10. Using a jar lifter, remove the jars and place them on a towel, leaving at least 1 inch of space between the jars during cooling. Let jars sit undisturbed to cool at room temperature for 12 to 24 hours.

Pressure canners

Pressure canners for use in the home have been extensively redesigned in recent years. Models made before the 1970s were heavy-walled kettles with clamp-on or turn-on lids. They were fitted with a dial gauge, a vent port in the form of a petcock or counterweight, and a safety fuse. Modern pressure canners are lightweight, thin-walled kettles; most have turn-on lids. They have a jar rack, gasket, dial or weighted gauge,

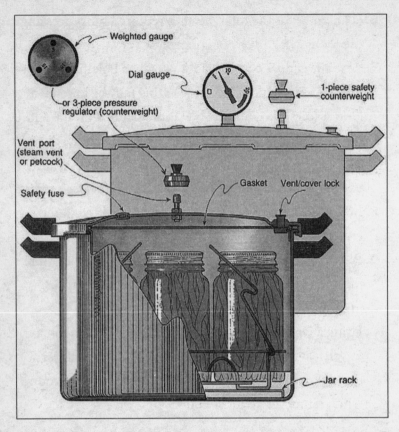

automatic vent/cover lock, vent port (steam vent) to be closed with a counterweight or weighted gauge, and safety fuse.

Pressure does not destroy microorganisms, but high temperatures applied for an adequate period of time do kill microorganisms. The success of destroying all microorganisms capable of growing in canned food is based on the temperature obtained in pure steam, free of air, at sea level.

At sea level, a canner that is operated at a gauge pressure of 10.5 pounds provides an internal temperature of 240°F.

Two serious errors in temperatures obtained in pressure canners occur because:

1. **Internal canner temperatures are lower at higher altitudes.** To correct this error, canners must be operated at the increased pressures specified in this publication for appropriate altitude ranges.

2. **Air trapped in a canner lowers the temperature obtained at 5, 10, or 15 pounds of pressure and results in underprocessing.** The highest volume of air trapped in a canner occurs in processing raw-packed foods in dial-gauge canners. These canners do not vent air during processing. To be safe, all types of pressure canners must be vented for 10 minutes before they are pressurized.

To vent a canner, leave the vent port uncovered on newer models or manually open petcocks on some older models. Heating the filled canner with its lid locked into place boils water and generates steam that escapes through the petcock or vent port. When steam first escapes, set a timer for 10 minutes. After venting 10 minutes, close the petcock or place the counterweight or weighted gauge over the vent port to pressurize the canner.

Weighted-gauge models exhaust tiny amounts of air and steam each time their gauge rocks or jiggles during processing. They control pressure precisely and need neither watching during processing nor checking for accuracy. The sound of the weight rocking or jiggling indicates that the canner is maintaining the recommended pressure. The single disadvantage of weighted-gauge canners is that they cannot correct precisely for higher altitudes. At altitudes above 1,000 feet, they must be operated at canner pressures of 10 instead of 5, or 15 instead of 10, PSI.

Check dial gauges for accuracy before use each year. Gauges that read high cause underprocessing and may result in unsafe food. Low readings cause overprocessing. Pressure adjustments can be made if the gauge reads up to 2 pounds high or low. Replace gauges that differ by more than 2 pounds. Every pound of pressure is very important to the temperature needed inside the canner for producing safe food, so accurate gauges and adjustments are essential when a gauge reads higher than it should. If a gauge is reading lower than it should, adjustments may be made to avoid overprocessing but are not essential to safety. Gauges may be checked at many county Cooperative Extension offices. Contact the pressure-canner manufacturer for other options.

Handle canner-lid gaskets carefully, and clean them according to the manufacturer's directions. Nicked or dried gaskets will allow steam leaks during pressurization of canners. Keep gaskets clean between uses. Gaskets on older-model canners may require a light coat of vegetable oil once per year. Gaskets on newer-model canners are prelubricated and do not benefit from oiling. Check your canner's instructions if there is doubt that the particular gasket you use has been prelubricated.

Lid safety fuses are thin metal inserts or rubber plugs designed to relieve excessive pressure from the canner. Do not pick at or scratch fuses while cleaning lids. Use only canners that have the Underwriter's Laboratory (UL) approval to ensure their safety.

Replacement gauges and other parts for canners are often available at stores offering canning equipment or from canner manufacturers. When ordering parts, give your canner model number and describe the parts needed.

Using pressure canners

Follow these steps for successful pressure canning:

1. Put 2 to 3 inches of hot water in the canner. Some specific products in this guide require that you start with even more water in the canner. Always follow the directions with USDA processes for specific foods if they require

more water added to the canner. Place filled jars on the rack using a jar lifter. When using a jar lifter, make sure it is securely positioned below the neck of the jar (below the screw band of the lid). Keep the jar upright at all times. Tilting the jar could cause food to spill into the sealing area of the lid. Fasten canner lid securely.

2. Leave the weight off the vent port, or open the petcock. Heat at the highest setting until steam flows freely from the open petcock or vent port.

3. While maintaining the high heat setting, let the steam flow (exhaust) continuously for 10 minutes, and then place the weight on the vent port or close the petcock. The canner will pressurize during the next 3 to 5 minutes.

4. Start timing the process when the pressure reading on the dial gauge indicates that the recommended pressure has been reached or when the weighted gauge begins to jiggle or rock as the canner manufacturer describes.

5. Regulate heat under the canner to maintain a steady pressure at or slightly above the correct gauge pressure. Quick and large pressure variations during processing may cause unnecessary liquid losses from jars. Follow the canner manufacturer's directions for how a weighted gauge should indicate it is maintaining the desired pressure.

IMPORTANT: If at any time the pressure goes below the recommended amount, bring the canner back up to the

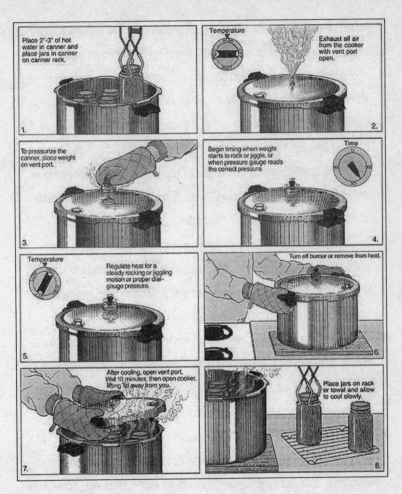

1. Place 2"-3" of hot water in canner and place jars in canner on canner rack.

2. Temperature. Exhaust all air from the cooker with vent port open.

3. To pressurize the canner, place weight on vent port.

4. Begin timing when weight starts to rock or jiggle, or when pressure gauge reads the correct pressure. Time

5. Temperature. Regulate heat for a steady rocking or jiggling motion or proper dial-gauge pressure.

6. Turn off burner or remove from heat.

7. After cooling, open vent port. Wait 10 minutes; then open cooker, lifting lid away from you.

8. Place jars on rack or towel and allow to cool slowly.

recommended pressure and begin the timing of the process over, from the beginning (using the total original process time). This is important for the safety of the food.

6. When the timed process is completed, turn off the heat, remove the canner from the heat if possible, and let the canner depressurize. Do not force-cool the canner. Forced cooling may result in unsafe food or food spoilage. Cooling the canner with cold running water or opening the vent port before the canner is fully depressurized will cause loss of liquid from jars and seal failures. Forced cooling may also warp the canner lid of older-model canners, causing steam leaks. Depressurization of older models without dial gauges should be timed. Standard-size heavy-walled canners require about 30 minutes when loaded with pints and 45 minutes with quarts. Newer thin-walled canners cool more rapidly and are equipped with vent locks. These canners are depressurized when their vent-lock piston drops to a normal position.

7. After the canner is depressurized, remove the weight from the vent port or open the petcock. Wait 10 minutes, unfasten the lid, and remove it carefully. Lift the lid away from you so that the steam does not burn your face.

8. Remove jars with a jar lifter, and place them on a towel, leaving at least 1 inch of space between the jars during cooling. Let jars sit undisturbed to cool at room temperature for 12 to 24 hours.

Selecting the correct processing time

When canning in boiling water, more processing time is

needed for most raw-packed foods and for quart jars than is needed for hot-packed foods and pint jars.

To destroy microorganisms in acid foods processed in a boiling-water canner, you must:

◆ Process the jars for the correct number of minutes in boiling water.
◆ Cool the jars at room temperature.

The food may spoil if you fail to add process time for lower boiling-water temperatures at altitudes above 1,000 feet, if you process the jars for fewer minutes than specified, or if you cool the jars in cold water.

To destroy microorganisms in low-acid foods processed with a pressure canner, you must:

◆ Process the jars using the correct time and pressure specified for your altitude.
◆ Allow the canner to cool at room temperature until it is completely depressurized.

The food may spoil if you select an improper process time for your altitude, fail to exhaust the canner properly, process at lower pressure than specified, process for fewer minutes than specified, or cool the canner with water.

Using tables for determining proper process time or pressure

This guide includes processing times with altitude adjustments for each product. Process times for half-pint and pint jars are the same, as are times for 1½-pint and quart jars. For some products, you have a choice of processing at 5, 10, or 15 PSI. In these cases, choose the canner pressure you wish to use and match it with your pack style (raw or hot) and jar size to find the correct process time. The following examples show how to select the proper process time or pressure for each type of canner. Process times are given in separate tables for sterilizing jars of food in boiling-water, dial-gauge, and weighted-gauge pressure canners.

Example A: Boiling-water canner

Suppose you are canning peaches as a hot pack in quarts at 2,500 feet above sea level, using a *boiling-water canner*. First, select the process table for boiling-water canner. The example for peaches is given in **Table for Example A** at the top of the next page. From that table, select the process time given for (1) the style of pack (hot), (2) the jar size (quarts), and (3) the altitude where you live (1,001–3,000 ft). You should have selected a process time of 30 minutes (min).

Table for Example A

Recommended process time for Peaches in a boiling-water canner

Style of pack	Jar size	0–1,000 ft	1,001–3,000 ft	3,001–6,000 ft	Above 6,000 ft
Hot	Pints	20 min	25 min	30 min	35 min
	Quarts	25	30	35	40
Raw	Pints	25	30	35	40
	Quarts	30	35	40	45

Column group header: Process time at Altitudes of

Example B: Dial-gauge pressure canner

Suppose you are canning peaches as a hot-pack in quarts at 2,500 feet above sea level, using a *dial-gauge pressure canner*. First, select the process table for dial-gauge pressure canner. The example for peaches is given in **Table for Example B** below. From that table, select the process pressure (PSI) given for (1) the style of pack (hot), (2) the jar size (quarts), (3) the process time in minutes (10 min), and (4) the altitude where you live (2,001–4,000 ft). You should have selected a pressure of 7 pounds (lb) for the 10-minute process time.

Table for Example B

Recommended process time for Peaches in a dial-gauge pressure canner

Style of pack	Jar size	Process Time	0–2,000 ft	2,001–4,000 ft	4,001–6,000 ft	6,001–8,000 ft
Hot or Raw	Pints or Quarts	10 min	6 lb	7 lb	8 lb	9 lb

Column group header: Canner Pressure (PSI) at Altitudes of

Example C: Weighted-gauge pressure canner

Suppose you are canning peaches as a hot-pack in quarts at 2,500 feet above sea level, using a *weighted-gauge pressure canner*. First, select the process table for weighted-gauge pressure canner. The example for peaches is given in **Table for Example C** below. From that table, select the process pressure (PSI) given for (1) the style of pack (hot), (2) the jar size (quarts), (3) the process time in minutes (10 min), and (4) the altitude where you live (Above 1,000 ft). You should have selected a pressure of 10 pounds (lb) for the 10-minute process time.

Table for Example C
Recommended process time for Peaches in a weighted-gauge pressure canner

Style of pack	Jar size	Process Time	Canner Pressure (PSI) at Altitudes of	
			0– 1,000 ft	Above 1,000 ft
Hot or Raw	Pints or Quarts	10 min	5 lb	10 lb

Cooling jars

When you remove hot jars from a canner, do not retighten their lids. Retightening of hot lids may cut through the gasket and cause seal failures. Cool the jars at room temperature for 12 to 24 hours. Jars may be cooled on racks or towels to minimize heat damage to counters. The food level and liquid volume of raw-packed jars will be noticeably

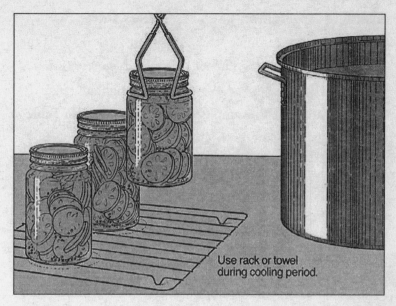

Use rack or towel during cooling period.

lower after cooling. During processing, air is exhausted and food shrinks. If a jar loses excessive liquid during processing, do not open it to add more liquid. Check for sealed lids as described below.

Testing jar seals

After cooling jars for 12 to 24 hours, remove the screw bands and test seals with one of the following options:

OPTION 1. Press the middle of the lid with a finger or thumb. If the lid springs up when you release your finger, the lid is unsealed.

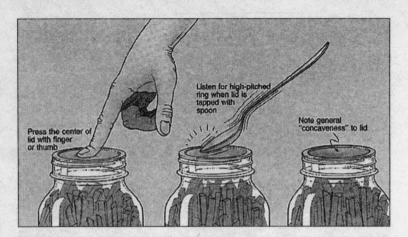

Press the center of lid with finger or thumb

Listen for high-pitched ring when lid is tapped with spoon

Note general "concaveness" to lid

OPTION 2. Tap the lid with the bottom of a teaspoon. If it makes a dull sound, the lid is not sealed. If food is in contact with the underside of the lid, it will also cause a dull sound. If the jar is sealed correctly, it will make a ringing, high-pitched sound.

OPTION 3. Hold the jar at eye level and look across the lid. The lid should be concave (curved down slightly in the center). If the center of the lid is either flat or bulging, it may not be sealed.

Reprocessing unsealed jars

If a lid fails to seal on a jar, remove the lid and check the jar-sealing surface for tiny nicks. If necessary, change the jar; add a new, properly prepared lid; and reprocess within 24 hours using the same processing time. Headspace in unsealed jars may be adjusted to 1½ inches, and jars could be frozen instead of reprocessed. Foods in single unsealed jars could be stored in the refrigerator and consumed within several days.

Storing canned foods

If lids are tightly vacuum-sealed on cooled jars, remove screw bands; wash the lid and jar to remove food residue; then rinse and dry jars. Label and date the jars, and store them in a clean, cool, dark, dry place. Do not store jars above 95°F or near hot pipes, a range, or a furnace; under a sink; in an uninsulated attic; or in direct sunlight. Under these conditions, food will lose quality in a few weeks or months and may spoil. Dampness may corrode metal lids, break seals, and allow recontamination and spoilage.

Accidental freezing of canned foods will not cause spoilage unless jars become unsealed and recontaminated. However, freezing and thawing may soften food. If jars must be stored where they may freeze, wrap them in newspapers, place them in heavy cartons, and cover with more newspapers and blankets.

Identifying and handling spoiled canned food

Do not taste food from a jar with an unsealed lid or food that shows signs of spoilage. You can more easily detect some types of spoilage in jars stored without screw bands. Growth of spoilage bacteria and yeast produces gas, which pressurizes the food, swells lids, and breaks jar seals. As each stored jar is selected for use, examine its lid for tightness and vacuum. Lids with concave centers have good seals.

Next, while holding the jar upright at eye level, rotate the jar and examine its outside surface for streaks of dried food originating at the top of the jar. Look at the contents for rising air bubbles and unnatural color.

While opening the jar, smell for unnatural odors and look for spurting liquid and cotton-like mold growth (white, blue, black, or green) on the top food surface and underside of lid.

Spoiled low-acid foods, including tomatoes, may exhibit different kinds of spoilage evidence or very little evidence. So, any container of low-acid food (including tomatoes) that you suspect is spoiled should be treated as having produced botulinum toxin and handled carefully in one of two ways:

✦ If the suspect glass jars or swollen metal cans are still sealed, place them in a heavy garbage bag. Close the bag and place it in a regular trash container or dispose of it in a nearby landfill.

✦ If the suspect glass jars or cans are unsealed, open, or leaking, they should be detoxified before disposal:

DETOXIFICATION PROCESS: Wear disposable rubber or heavy-plastic gloves. Carefully place the suspect containers and lids on their sides in an 8-quart-volume or larger stock pot, pan, or boiling-water canner. With your hands still in the gloves, thoroughly wash the outside surface of the gloves. Carefully add water to the pot and avoid splashing the water. The water should completely cover the containers with a minimum of a 1-inch level above the containers. Place a lid on the pot and heat the water to boiling. Boil 30 minutes to ensure detoxification of food and all container components. Cool and discard the containers, their lids, and the food in the trash or dispose of them in a nearby landfill.

CLEANING UP THE AREA: Contact with botulinum toxin can be fatal whether it is ingested or enters through the skin. Take care to avoid contact with suspect foods or liquids. Wear rubber or heavy-plastic gloves when handling suspect foods or cleaning up contaminated work surfaces and equipment. A fresh solution of 1 part unscented liquid household chlorine bleach (5 percent to 6 percent sodium hypochlorite) to 5 parts clean water should be used to treat work surfaces, equipment, or other items, including can openers and clothing, that may have come in contact with suspect foods or liquids. Spray or wet contaminated surfaces with the bleach solution and let stand for 30 minutes. Wearing gloves, wipe up treated spills with paper towels, being careful to minimize the spread of contamination. Dispose of these paper towels by placing them in a plastic bag before putting them in the trash. Next, apply the bleach solution to all surfaces and equipment again, let stand for 30 minutes, and rinse. As a last step, thoroughly wash all detoxified counters, containers, equipment, clothing, etc. Discard gloves when cleaning process is complete. (Note: Bleach itself is an irritant and should not be inhaled or allowed to come in contact with the skin.)

Preparing pickled and fermented foods

The many varieties of pickled and fermented foods are classified by ingredients and method of preparation.

Regular dill pickles and sauerkraut are fermented and cured for about 3 weeks. Refrigerator dills are fermented for about 1 week. During curing, colors and flavors change and acidity increases. Fresh-pack or quick-process pickles are not fermented; some are brined several hours or overnight, then drained and covered with vinegar and seasonings. Fruit pickles usually are prepared by heating fruit in a seasoned syrup acidified with either lemon juice or vinegar. Relishes are made from chopped fruits and vegetables that are cooked with seasonings and vinegar.

Be sure to remove and discard a $\frac{1}{16}$-inch slice from the blossom end of fresh cucumbers. Blossoms may contain an enzyme that causes excessive softening of pickles.

Caution: The level of acidity in a pickled product is as important to its safety as it is to taste and texture.

❖ **Do not alter vinegar, food, or water proportions in a recipe or use a vinegar with unknown acidity.**

❖ **Use only recipes with tested proportions of ingredients.**

❖ **There must be a minimum, uniform level of acid throughout the mixed product to prevent the growth of botulinum bacteria.**

Ingredients

Select fresh, firm fruits or vegetables free of spoilage. Measure or weigh amounts carefully, because the proportion of fresh food to other ingredients will affect flavor and, in many instances, safety.

Use canning or pickling salt. Noncaking material added to other salts may make the brine cloudy. Since flake salt varies in density, it is not recommended for making pickled and fermented foods. White-granulated and brown sugars are most often used. Corn syrup and honey, unless called for in reliable recipes, may produce undesirable flavors. White-distilled and cider vinegars of 5 percent acidity (50 grain) are recommended. White vinegar is usually preferred when light color is desirable, as is the case with fruits and cauliflower.

Pickles with reduced salt content

Recipes for pickles with reduced sodium content are provided in Chapter 3.

In the making of fresh-pack pickles, cucumbers are acidified quickly with vinegar. Use only tested recipes formulated to produce the proper acidity. While these pickles may be prepared safely with reduced or no salt, their quality may be noticeably lower. Both texture and flavor may be slightly, but noticeably, different than expected. You may wish to make small quantities first to determine if you like them.

However, the salt used in making fermented sauerkraut and brined pickles not only provides characteristic flavor but also is vital to safety and texture. In fermented foods, salt favors the growth of desirable bacteria while inhibiting the growth of others. **Caution: Do not attempt to make sauerkraut or fermented pickles by cutting back on the salt required.**

Firming agents

Alum may be safely used to firm fermented pickles. However, it is unnecessary and is not included in the recipes in this publication. Alum does not improve the firmness of quick-process pickles. The calcium in lime definitely improves pickle firmness. Food-grade lime may be used as a lime-water solution for soaking fresh cucumbers 12 to 24 hours before pickling them. Excess lime absorbed by the cucumbers must be removed to make safe pickles. To remove excess lime, drain the lime-water solution, rinse, and then resoak the cucumbers in fresh water for 1 hour. Repeat the rinsing and soaking steps 2 more times. To further improve pickle firmness, you may process cucumber pickles for 30 minutes in water at 180°F. This process also prevents spoilage, **but the water temperature should not fall below 180°F.** Use a candy or jelly thermometer to check the water temperature.

Preventing spoilage

Pickled products are subject to spoilage from microorganisms, particularly yeasts and molds, as well as enzymes that may affect flavor, color, and texture. Processing the pickles in a boiling-water canner will prevent both of these problems. Standard canning jars and self-sealing lids are recommended. Processing times and procedures will vary according to food acidity and the size of food pieces.

Canned foods for special diets

The cost of commercially canned foods for special diets often prompts interest in preparing these products at home instead. Some low-sugar and low-salt foods may be easily and safely canned at home. However, the color, flavor, and texture of these foods may be different than expected and less acceptable.

Canning without salt (reduced sodium)

To can reduced-sodium vegetables, use the procedures given in Chapter 3, but omit the salt. In these products, salt seasons the food but is not necessary to ensure its safety. Add salt substitutes, if desired, when serving.

Canning baby foods

Caution: Do not attempt to can pureed vegetables, red meats, or poultry meats, because proper processing times for pureed foods have not been determined for home use. Instead, can and store these vegetables using the standard processing procedures, and then puree or blend them at serving time. Heat the blended foods to boiling, simmer for 10 minutes, cool, and serve. Store unused portions in the refrigerator and use within 2 days for best quality.

Chapter 2

Selecting, Preparing, and Canning Vegetables and Vegetable Products

Asparagus—Spears or Pieces

Quantity: An average of 24½ pounds is needed per canner load of 7 quarts; an average of 16 pounds is needed per canner load of 9 pints. A crate weighs 31 pounds and yields 7 to 12 quarts—an average of 3½ pounds per quart.

Quality: Use tender, tight-tipped spears, 4 to 6 inches long.

Procedure: Wash asparagus and trim off tough scales. Break off tough stems and wash again. Cut into 1-inch pieces or can whole.

HOT PACK—Cover asparagus with boiling water. Boil 2 or 3 minutes. Loosely fill hot jars with hot asparagus, leaving 1 inch of headspace.

RAW PACK—Fill hot jars with raw asparagus, packing as tightly as possible without crushing, leaving 1 inch of headspace.

Add 1 teaspoon of salt per quart to the jars, if desired. Add boiling water, leaving 1 inch of headspace. Remove air bubbles and adjust headspace if needed. Wipe rims of jars with a dampened, clean paper towel. Adjust lids, and process.

Asparagus

Recommended process time for Asparagus in a dial-gauge pressure canner

Style of pack	Jar size	Process Time	Canner Pressure (PSI) at Altitudes of			
			0–2,000 ft	2,001–4,000 ft	4,001–6,000 ft	6,001–8,000 ft
Hot or Raw	Pints	30 min	11 lb	12 lb	13 lb	14 lb
	Quarts	40	11	12	13	14

Asparagus

Recommended process time for Asparagus in a weighted-gauge pressure canner

Style of pack	Jar size	Process Time	Canner Pressure (PSI) at Altitudes of	
			0–1,000 ft	Above 1,000 ft
Hot or Raw	Pints	30 min	10 lb	15 lb
	Quarts	40	10	15

Beans or Peas—Shelled, Dried

All varieties

Quantity: An average of 5 pounds is needed per canner load of 7 quarts; an average of 3¼ pounds is needed per canner load of 9 pints—an average of ¾ pound per quart.

Quality: Select mature, dry seeds. Sort out and discard discolored seeds.

Procedure: Place dried beans or peas in a large pot, and cover with water. Soak 12 to 18 hours in a cool place. Drain water. To more quickly hydrate beans, you may instead cover sorted and washed beans with boiling water in a saucepan. Boil 2 minutes, remove from heat, soak 1 hour, and drain. Cover beans soaked by either method with fresh water and boil 30 minutes. Add ½ teaspoon of salt per pint or 1 teaspoon per quart to the jar, if desired. Fill hot jars with hot beans or peas and cooking water, leaving 1 inch of headspace. Remove air bubbles and adjust headspace if needed. Wipe rims of jars with a dampened, clean paper towel. Adjust lids, and process.

Beans or Peas

Recommended process time for Beans or Peas in a dial-gauge pressure canner

Style of pack	Jar size	Process Time	Canner Pressure (PSI) at Altitudes of			
			0–2,000 ft	2,001–4,000 ft	4,001–6,000 ft	6,001–8,000 ft
Hot	Pints	75 min	11 lb	12 lb	13 lb	14 lb
	Quarts	90	11	12	13	14

Beans or Peas

Recommended process time for Beans or Peas in a weighted-gauge pressure canner

Style of pack	Jar size	Process Time	Canner Pressure (PSI) at Altitudes of	
			0–1,000 ft	Above 1,000 ft
Hot	Pints	75 min	10 lb	15 lb
	Quarts	90	10	15

Beans, Baked

Procedure: Soak and boil beans and prepare molasses sauce according to directions for "Beans, Dry, with Tomato or Molasses Sauce" on pages 58–59. Place seven ¾-inch-long pieces of pork, ham, or bacon in an earthenware crock or large casserole.

Add beans and enough molasses sauce to cover beans. Cover and bake 4 to 5 hours at 350°F. Add water as needed—about every hour. Fill hot jars, leaving 1 inch of headspace. Remove air bubbles and adjust headspace if needed. Wipe rims of jars with a dampened, clean paper towel. Adjust lids, and process as for "Beans, Dry, with Tomato or Molasses Sauce."

Beans, Dry, with Tomato or Molasses Sauce

Quantity: An average of 5 pounds of beans is needed per canner load of 7 quarts; an average of 3¼ pounds is needed per canner load of 9 pints—an average of ¾ pound per quart.

Quality: Select mature, dry seeds. Sort out and discard discolored seeds.

Procedure: Sort and wash dry beans. Add 3 cups of water for each cup of dried beans. Boil 2 minutes, remove from heat, soak 1 hour, and drain. Heat to boiling in fresh water, and save liquid for making sauce. Make your choice of the following sauces:

TOMATO SAUCE—Either mix 1 quart tomato juice, 3 tablespoons sugar, 2 teaspoons salt, 1 tablespoon chopped onion, and ¼ teaspoon each of ground cloves, allspice, mace, and cayenne pepper; or, mix 1 cup tomato ketchup with 3 cups of cooking liquid from beans. Heat to boiling.

MOLASSES SAUCE—Mix 4 cups water or cooking liquid from beans, 3 tablespoons dark molasses, 1 tablespoon vinegar, 2 teaspoons salt, and ¾ teaspoon powdered dry mustard. Heat to boiling.

Fill hot jars three-fourths full with hot beans. Add a ¾-inch cube of pork, ham, or bacon to each jar, if desired. Fill jars with heated sauce, leaving 1 inch of headspace. Remove air bubbles and adjust headspace if needed. Wipe rims of jars with a dampened, clean paper towel. Adjust lids, and process.

Beans, Dry, with Tomato or Molasses Sauce

Recommended process time for Dry Beans with Tomato or Molasses Sauce in a dial-gauge pressure canner

Style of pack	Jar size	Process Time	Canner Pressure (PSI) at Altitudes of			
			0–2,000 ft	2,001–4,000 ft	4,001–6,000 ft	6,001–8,000 ft
Hot	Pints	65 min	11 lb	12 lb	13 lb	14 lb
	Quarts	75	11	12	13	14

Beans, Dry, with Tomato or Molasses Sauce

Recommended process time for Dry Beans with Tomato or Molasses Sauce in a weighted-gauge pressure canner

Style of pack	Jar size	Process Time	Canner Pressure (PSI) at Altitudes of	
			0–1,000 ft	Above 1,000 ft
Hot	Pints	65 min	10 lb	15 lb
	Quarts	75	10	15

Beans, Fresh Lima—Shelled

Quantity: An average of 28 pounds is needed per canner load of 7 quarts; an average of 18 pounds is needed per canner load of 9 pints. A bushel weighs 32 pounds and yields 6 to 10 quarts—an average of 4 pounds per quart.

Quality: Select well-filled pods with green seeds. Discard insect-damaged and diseased seeds.

Procedure: Shell beans and wash thoroughly.

HOT PACK—Cover beans with boiling water, and heat to boil. Fill hot jars loosely, leaving 1 inch of headspace.

RAW PACK—Fill hot jars with raw beans. Do not press or shake down.

> Small beans—leave 1 inch of headspace for pints and 1½ inches for quarts.
> Large beans—leave 1 inch of headspace for pints and 1¼ inches for quarts.

Add 1 teaspoon of salt per quart to the jar, if desired. Add boiling water, leaving the same headspaces listed above. Remove air bubbles and adjust headspace if needed. Wipe rims of jars with a dampened, clean paper towel. Adjust lids, and process.

Lima Beans

Recommended process time for Lima Beans in a dial-gauge pressure canner

Style of pack	Jar size	Process Time	Canner Pressure (PSI) at Altitudes of			
			0–2,000 ft	2,001–4,000 ft	4,001–6,000 ft	6,001–8,000 ft
Hot or Raw	Pints	40 min	11 lb	12 lb	13 lb	14 lb
	Quarts	50	11	12	13	14

Lima Beans

Recommended process time for Lima Beans in a weighted-gauge pressure canner

Style of pack	Jar size	Process Time	Canner Pressure (PSI) at Altitudes of	
			0–1,000 ft	Above 1,000 ft
Hot or Raw	Pints	40 min	10 lb	15 lb
	Quarts	50	10	15

Beans, Snap or Italian—Pieces

Green and wax

Quantity: An average of 14 pounds is needed per canner load of 7 quarts; an average of 9 pounds is needed per canner load of 9 pints. A bushel weighs 30 pounds and yields 12 to 20 quarts—an average of 2 pounds per quart.

Quality: Select filled but tender, crisp pods. Remove and discard diseased and rusty pods.

Procedure: Wash beans and trim ends. Leave whole, or cut or snap into 1-inch pieces.

HOT PACK—Cover with boiling water; boil 5 minutes. Fill hot jars loosely, leaving 1 inch of headspace.

RAW PACK—Fill hot jars tightly with raw beans, leaving 1 inch of headspace.

Add 1 teaspoon of canning salt per quart to the jar, if desired. Add boiling water, leaving 1 inch of headspace. Remove air bubbles and adjust headspace if needed. Wipe rims of jars with a dampened, clean paper towel. Adjust lids, and process.

Snap or Italian Beans

Recommended process time for Snap or Italian Beans in a dial-gauge pressure canner

Style of pack	Jar size	Process Time	Canner Pressure (PSI) at Altitudes of			
			0–2,000 ft	2,001–4,000 ft	4,001–6,000 ft	6,001–8,000 ft
Hot or Raw	Pints	20 min	11 lb	12 lb	13 lb	14 lb
	Quarts	25	11	12	13	14

Snap or Italian Beans

Recommended process time for Snap or Italian Beans in a weighted-gauge pressure canner

Style of pack	Jar size	Process Time	Canner Pressure (PSI) at Altitudes of	
			0–1,000 ft	Above 1,000 ft
Hot or Raw	Pints	20 min	10 lb	15 lb
	Quarts	25	10	15

Beets—Whole, Cubed, or Sliced

Quantity: An average of 21 pounds (without tops) is needed per canner load of 7 quarts; an average of 13½ pounds is needed per canner load of 9 pints. A bushel (without tops) weighs 52 pounds and yields 15 to 20 quarts—an average of 3 pounds per quart.

Quality: Beets with a diameter of 1 to 2 inches are preferred for whole packs. Beets larger than 3 inches in diameter are often fibrous.

Procedure: Trim off beet tops, leaving an inch of stem and roots to reduce bleeding of color. Scrub well. Cover with boiling water. Boil until skins slip off easily—about 15 to 25 minutes depending on size. Cool, remove skins, and trim off stems and roots. Leave baby beets whole. Cut medium or large beets into ½-inch cubes or slices. Halve or quarter very large slices. Add 1 teaspoon of salt per quart to the jar, if desired. Fill hot jars with hot beets and fresh hot water, leaving 1 inch of headspace. Remove air bubbles and adjust headspace if needed. Wipe rims of jars with a dampened, clean paper towel. Adjust lids, and process.

Beets

Recommended process time for Beets in a dial-gauge pressure canner

Style of pack	Jar size	Process Time	Canner Pressure (PSI) at Altitudes of			
			0–2,000 ft	2,001–4,000 ft	4,001–6,000 ft	6,001–8,000 ft
Hot	Pints	30 min	11 lb	12 lb	13 lb	14 lb
	Quarts	35	11	12	13	14

Beets

Recommended process time for Beets in a weighted-gauge pressure canner

Style of pack	Jar size	Process Time	Canner Pressure (PSI) at Altitudes of	
			0–1,000 ft	Above 1,000 ft
Hot	Pints	30 min	10 lb	15 lb
	Quarts	35	10	15

Carrots—Sliced or Diced

Quantity: An average of 17½ pounds (without tops) is needed per canner load of 7 quarts; an average of 11 pounds (without tops) is needed per canner load of 9 pints. A bushel (without tops) weighs 50 pounds and yields 17 to 25 quarts—an average of 2½ pounds per quart.

Quality: Select small carrots, preferably 1 to 1¼ inches in diameter. Larger carrots are often too fibrous.

Procedure: Wash, peel, and rewash carrots. Slice or dice.

HOT PACK—Cover with boiling water; bring to boil and simmer for 5 minutes. Fill hot jars, leaving 1 inch of headspace.

RAW PACK—Fill hot jars tightly with raw carrots, leaving 1 inch of headspace.

Add 1 teaspoon of salt per quart to the jar, if desired. Add hot cooking liquid or water, leaving 1 inch of headspace. Remove air bubbles and adjust headspace if needed. Wipe rims of jars with a dampened, clean paper towel. Adjust lids, and process.

Carrots

Recommended process time for Carrots in a dial-gauge pressure canner

Style of pack	Jar size	Process Time	Canner Pressure (PSI) at Altitudes of			
			0–2,000 ft	2,001–4,000 ft	4,001–6,000 ft	6,001–8,000 ft
Hot or Raw	Pints	25 min	11 lb	12 lb	13 lb	14 lb
	Quarts	30	11	12	13	14

Carrots

Recommended process time for Carrots in a weighted-gauge pressure canner

Style of pack	Jar size	Process Time	Canner Pressure (PSI) at Altitudes of	
			0–1,000 ft	Above 1,000 ft
Hot or Raw	Pints	25 min	10 lb	15 lb
	Quarts	30	10	15

Corn—Cream Style

Quantity: An average of 20 pounds (in husks) of sweet corn is needed per canner load of 9 pints. A bushel weighs 35 pounds and yields 12 to 20 pints—an average of 2¼ pounds per pint.

Quality: Select ears containing slightly immature kernels or ears of ideal quality for eating fresh.

Procedure: Husk corn, remove silk, and wash ears. Blanch ears 4 minutes in boiling water. Cut corn from cob at about the center of the kernel. Scrape remaining corn from cobs with a table knife.

HOT PACK—To each quart of corn and scrapings, in a saucepan, add 2 cups of boiling water. Heat to boiling. Add ½ teaspoon salt to each jar, if desired. Fill hot pint jar with hot corn mixture, leaving 1 inch of headspace. Remove air bubbles and adjust headspace if needed. Wipe rims of jars with a dampened, clean paper towel. Adjust lids, and process.

Cream-Style Corn

Recommended process time for Cream-Style Corn in a dial-gauge pressure canner

Style of pack	Jar size	Process Time	Canner Pressure (PSI) at Altitudes of			
			0–2,000 ft	2,001–4,000 ft	4,001–6,000 ft	6,001–8,000 ft
Hot	Pints	85 min	11 lb	12 lb	13 lb	14 lb

Cream-Style Corn

Recommended process time for Cream-Style Corn in a weighted-gauge pressure canner

Style of pack	Jar size	Process Time	Canner Pressure (PSI) at Altitudes of	
			0–1,000 ft	Above 1,000 ft
Hot	Pints	85 min	10 lb	15 lb

Corn—Whole Kernel

Quantity: An average of 31½ pounds (in husks) of sweet corn is needed per canner load of 7 quarts; an average of 20 pounds is needed per canner load of 9 pints. A bushel weighs 35 pounds and yields 6 to 11 quarts—an average of 4½ pounds per quart.

Quality: Select ears containing slightly immature kernels or ears of ideal quality for eating fresh. Canning of some sweeter varieties or of kernels that are too immature may cause browning. Before canning large quantities, can a small amount and check color and flavor.

Procedure: Husk corn, remove silk, and wash. Blanch 3 minutes in boiling water. Cut corn from cob at about ¾ the depth of the kernel.

Caution: Do not scrape cob.

HOT PACK—To each clean quart of kernels in a saucepan, add 1 cup of hot water, heat to boiling, and simmer 5 minutes. Add 1 teaspoon of salt per quart to the jar, if desired. Fill hot jars with corn and cooking liquid, leaving 1 inch of headspace.

RAW PACK—Fill hot jars with raw kernels, leaving 1 inch of headspace. Do not shake or press down. Add 1 teaspoon of salt per quart to the jar, if desired.

Add fresh boiling water, leaving 1 inch of headspace. Remove air bubbles and adjust headspace if needed. Wipe rims of jars with a dampened, clean paper towel. Adjust lids, and process according to the tables at the top of the next page.

Whole-Kernel Corn

Recommended process time for Whole-Kernel Corn in a dial-gauge pressure canner

Style of pack	Jar size	Process Time	Canner Pressure (PSI) at Altitudes of			
			0–2,000 ft	2,001–4,000 ft	4,001–6,000 ft	6,001–8,000 ft
Hot or Raw	Pints	55 min	11 lb	12 lb	13 lb	14 lb
	Quarts	85	11	12	13	14

Whole-Kernel Corn

Recommended process time for Whole-Kernel Corn in a weighted-gauge pressure canner

Style of pack	Jar size	Process Time	Canner Pressure (PSI) at Altitudes of	
			0–1,000 ft	Above 1,000 ft
Hot or Raw	Pints	55 min	10 lb	15 lb
	Quarts	85	10	15

Mixed Vegetables

6 cups sliced carrots

6 cups cut, whole-kernel sweet corn

6 cups cut green beans

6 cups shelled lima beans

4 cups whole or crushed tomatoes

4 cups diced zucchini

YIELD: 7 quarts

Optional mix—You may change the suggested proportions or substitute other favorite vegetables except leafy greens, dried beans, cream-style corn, squash, or sweet potatoes.

Procedure: Except for zucchini, wash and prepare vegetables as described in individual vegetable profiles. (For tomato preparation, see page 81 of accompanying guide *How to Prepare & Can Fruits, Jams, Jellies & More.*) Wash, trim, and slice or cube zucchini. Combine all vegetables in a large pot or kettle, and add enough water to cover pieces. Add 1 teaspoon salt per quart to the jar, if desired. Boil 5 minutes and fill hot jars with hot pieces and liquid, leaving 1 inch of headspace. Remove air bubbles and adjust headspace if needed. Wipe rims of jars with a dampened, clean paper towel. Adjust lids, and process.

Mixed Vegetables

Recommended process time for Mixed Vegetables in a dial-gauge pressure canner

Style of pack	Jar size	Process Time	Canner Pressure (PSI) at Altitudes of			
			0–2,000 ft	2,001–4,000 ft	4,001–6,000 ft	6,001–8,000 ft
Hot	Pints	75 min	11 lb	12 lb	13 lb	14 lb
	Quarts	90	11	12	13	14

Mixed Vegetables

Recommended process time for Mixed Vegetables in a weighted-gauge pressure canner

Style of pack	Jar size	Process Time	Canner Pressure (PSI) at Altitudes of	
			0–1,000 ft	Above 1,000 ft
Hot	Pints	75 min	10 lb	15 lb
	Quarts	90	10	15

Mushrooms—Whole or Siced

Quantity: An average of 14½ pounds is needed per canner load of 9 pints; an average of 7½ pounds is needed per canner load of 9 half-pints—an average of 2 pounds per pint.

Quality: Select only brightly colored, small- to medium-size, domestic mushrooms with short stems, tight veils (unopened caps), and no discoloration.

Caution: Do not can wild mushrooms.

Procedure: Trim stems and discolored parts. Soak in cold water for 10 minutes to remove dirt. Wash in clean water. Leave small mushrooms whole; cut large ones. Cover with water in a saucepan and boil 5 minutes. Fill hot jars with hot mushrooms, leaving 1 inch of headspace. Add ½ teaspoon of salt per pint to the jar, if desired. For better color, add ⅛ teaspoon of ascorbic acid powder or a 500-milligram tablet of vitamin C. Add fresh hot water, leaving 1 inch of headspace. Remove air bubbles and adjust headspace if needed. Wipe rims of jars with a dampened, clean paper towel. Adjust lids, and process according to the table below or the one at the top of the next page.

Mushrooms

Recommended process time for Mushrooms in a dial-gauge pressure canner

Style of pack	Jar size	Process Time	Canner Pressure (PSI) at Altitudes of			
			0–2,000 ft	2,001–4,000 ft	4,001–6,000 ft	6,001–8,000 ft
Hot	Half-pints or Pints	45 min	11 lb	12 lb	13 lb	14 lb

Mushrooms

Recommended process time for Mushrooms in a weighted-gauge pressure canner

Style of pack	Jar size	Process Time	Canner Pressure (PSI) at Altitudes of	
			0–1,000 ft	Above 1,000 ft
Hot	Half-pints or Pints	45 min	10 lb	15 lb

Okra

Quantity: An average of 11 pounds is needed per canner load of 7 quarts; an average of 7 pounds is needed per canner load of 9 pints. A bushel weighs 26 pounds and yields 16 to 18 quarts—an average of 1½ pounds per quart.

Quality: Select young, tender pods. Remove and discard diseased and rust-spotted pods.

Procedure: Wash pods and trim ends. Leave whole or cut into 1-inch pieces. Cover with hot water in a saucepan, boil 2 minutes, and drain. Fill hot jars with hot okra and cooking liquid, leaving 1 inch of headspace. Add 1 teaspoon of salt per quart to the jar, if desired. Remove air bubbles and adjust headspace if needed. Wipe rims of jars with a dampened, clean paper towel. Adjust lids, and process.

Okra

Recommended process time for Okra in a dial-gauge pressure canner

Style of pack	Jar size	Process Time	Canner Pressure (PSI) at Altitudes of			
			0–2,000 ft	2,001–4,000 ft	4,001–6,000 ft	6,001–8,000 ft
Hot	Pints	25 min	11 lb	12 lb	13 lb	14 lb
	Quarts	40	11	12	13	14

Okra

Recommended process time for Okra in a weighted-gauge pressure canner

Style of pack	Jar size	Process Time	Canner Pressure (PSI) at Altitudes of	
			0–1,000 ft	Above 1,000 ft
Hot	Pints	25 min	10 lb	15 lb
	Quarts	40	10	15

Peas, Green or English—Shelled

It is recommended that sugar snap and Chinese edible pods be frozen, not canned, for best quality.

Quantity: An average of 31½ pounds (in pods) is needed per canner load of 7 quarts; an average of 20 pounds is needed per canner load of 9 pints. A bushel weighs 30 pounds and yields 5 to 10 quarts—an average of 4½ pounds per quart.

Quality: Select filled pods containing young, tender, sweet seeds. Discard diseased pods.

Procedure: Shell and wash peas. Add 1 teaspoon of salt per quart to the jar, if desired.

HOT PACK—Cover with boiling water. Bring to a boil in a saucepan, and boil 2 minutes. Fill hot jars loosely with hot peas and add cooking liquid, leaving 1 inch of headspace.

RAW PACK—Fill hot jars with raw peas and add boiling water, leaving 1 inch of headspace. Do not shake or press down peas.

Remove air bubbles and adjust headspace if needed. Wipe rims of jars with a dampened, clean paper towel. Adjust lids, and process.

Green or English Peas

Recommended process time for Green or English Peas in a dial-gauge pressure canner

Style of pack	Jar size	Process Time	Canner Pressure (PSI) at Altitudes of			
			0–2,000 ft	2,001–4,000 ft	4,001–6,000 ft	6,001–8,000 ft
Hot or Raw	Pints or Quarts	40 min	11 lb	12 lb	13 lb	14 lb

Green or English Peas

Recommended process time for Green or English Peas in a weighted-gauge pressure canner

Style of pack	Jar size	Process Time	Canner Pressure (PSI) at Altitudes of	
			0–1,000 ft	Above 1,000 ft
Hot or Raw	Pints or Quarts	40 min	10 lb	15 lb

Peppers
Hot or sweet, including chiles, jalapeños, and pimientos

Quantity: An average of 9 pounds is needed per canner load of 9 pints. A bushel weighs 25 pounds and yields 20 to 30 pints—an average of 1 pound per pint.

Quality: Select firm yellow, green, or red peppers. Do not use soft or diseased peppers.

Procedure: Select your favorite pepper(s). **Caution: If you choose hot peppers, wear plastic or rubber gloves and do not touch your face while handling or cutting hot peppers. If you do not wear gloves, wash hands thoroughly with soap and water before touching your face or eyes.** Small peppers may be left whole. Large peppers may be quartered. Remove cores and seeds. Slash two or four slits in each pepper, and either blanch in boiling water or blister skins using one of these two methods:

Oven or broiler method to blister skins—Place peppers in a hot oven (400°F) or broiler for 6 to 8 minutes until skins blister.

Range-top method to blister skins—Cover hot burner, either gas or electric, with heavy wire mesh. Place peppers on mesh-covered burner for several minutes until skins blister.

After blistering skins, place peppers in a pan and cover with a damp cloth. (This will make peeling the peppers easier.) Cool several minutes; peel off skins. Flatten whole peppers. Add ½ teaspoon of salt to each pint jar, if desired. Fill hot jars loosely with peppers and add fresh boiling water, leaving 1 inch of headspace. Remove air bubbles and adjust headspace if needed. Wipe rims of jars with a dampened, clean paper towel. Adjust lids, and process.

Peppers

Recommended process time for Peppers in a dial-gauge pressure canner

Style of pack	Jar size	Process Time	Canner Pressure (PSI) at Altitudes of			
			0–2,000 ft	2,001–4,000 ft	4,001–6,000 ft	6,001–8,000 ft
Hot	Half-pints or Pints	35 min	11 lb	12 lb	13 lb	14 lb

Peppers

Recommended process time for Peppers in a weighted-gauge pressure canner

Style of pack	Jar size	Process Time	Canner Pressure (PSI) at Altitudes of	
			0–1,000 ft	Above 1,000 ft
Hot	Half-pints or Pints	35 min	10 lb	15 lb

Potatoes, Sweet—Pieces or Whole

It is not recommended to dry-pack sweet potatoes.

Quantity: An average of 17½ pounds is needed per canner load of 7 quarts; an average of 11 pounds is needed per canner load of 9 pints. A bushel weighs 50 pounds and yields 17 to 25 quarts—an average of 2½ pounds per quart.

Quality: Choose small- to medium-size potatoes. They should be mature and not too fibrous. Can within 1 to 2 months after harvest.

Procedure: Wash potatoes and boil or steam until partially soft (15 to 20 minutes). Remove skins. Cut medium potatoes, if needed, so that pieces are uniform in size. **Caution: Do not mash or puree pieces.** Fill hot jars, leaving 1 inch of headspace. Add 1 teaspoon salt per quart to the jar, if desired. Cover with fresh boiling water, leaving 1 inch of headspace. Remove air bubbles and adjust headspace if needed. Wipe rims of jars with a dampened, clean paper towel. Adjust lids, and process.

Sweet Potatoes

Recommended process time for Sweet Potatoes in a dial-gauge pressure canner

Style of pack	Jar size	Process Time	Canner Pressure (PSI) at Altitudes of			
			0–2,000 ft	2,001–4,000 ft	4,001–6,000 ft	6,001–8,000 ft
Hot	Pints	65 min	11 lb	12 lb	13 lb	14 lb
	Quarts	90	11	12	13	14

Sweet Potatoes

Recommended process time for Sweet Potatoes in a weighted-gauge pressure canner

Style of pack	Jar size	Process Time	Canner Pressure (PSI) at Altitudes of	
			0–1,000 ft	Above 1,000 ft
Hot	Pints	65 min	10 lb	15 lb
	Quarts	90	10	15

Potatoes, White—Cubed or Whole

Quantity: An average of 20 pounds of potatoes is needed per canner load of 7 quarts; an average of 13 pounds is needed per canner load of 9 pints. A 50-pound bag yields 18 to 22 quarts—an average of 2½ to 3 pounds per quart.

Quality: Select small- to medium-size mature potatoes of ideal quality for cooking. Tubers stored below 45°F may discolor when canned. Choose potatoes 1 to 2 inches in diameter if they are to be packed whole.

Procedure: Wash and peel potatoes. Place in ascorbic acid solution to prevent darkening (see pages 19–20). If desired, cut into ½-inch cubes. Drain. Cook 2 minutes in boiling water and drain again. For whole potatoes, boil 10 minutes and drain. Add 1 teaspoon of salt per quart to the jar, if desired. Fill hot jars with hot potatoes and fresh hot water, leaving 1 inch of head-space. Remove air bubbles and adjust headspace if needed. Wipe rims of jars with a dampened, clean paper towel. Adjust lids, and process.

White Potatoes

Recommended process time for White Potatoes in a dial-gauge pressure canner

Style of pack	Jar size	Process Time	Canner Pressure (PSI) at Altitudes of			
			0–2,000 ft	2,001–4,000 ft	4,001–6,000 ft	6,001–8,000 ft
Hot	Pints	35 min	11 lb	12 lb	13 lb	14 lb
	Quarts	40	11	12	13	14

White Potatoes

Recommended process time for White Potatoes in a weighted-gauge pressure canner

Style of pack	Jar size	Process Time	Canner Pressure (PSI) at Altitudes of	
			0–1,000 ft	Above 1,000 ft
Hot	Pints	35 min	10 lb	15 lb
	Quarts	40	10	15

Pumpkins and Winter Squash—Cubed

Quantity: An average of 16 pounds is needed per canner load of 7 quarts; an average of 10 pounds is needed per canner load of 9 pints—an average of 2¼ pounds per quart.

Quality: Pumpkins and squash should have a hard rind and stringless, mature pulp of ideal quality for cooking fresh. Small-size pumpkins (sugar or pie varieties) make better products.

Procedure: Wash, remove seeds, cut into 1-inch-wide slices, and peel. Cut flesh into 1-inch cubes. Boil 2 minutes in water. **Caution: Do not mash or puree.** Fill hot jars with cubes and cooking liquid, leaving 1 inch of headspace. Remove air bubbles and adjust headspace if needed. Wipe rims of jars with a dampened, clean paper towel. Adjust lids, and process according to the tables at the top of the next page.

For making pies, drain jars and strain or sieve the cubes at pie-preparation time.

Pumpkins and Winter Squash

Recommended process time for Pumpkins and Winter Squash in a dial-gauge pressure canner

Style of pack	Jar size	Process Time	Canner Pressure (PSI) at Altitudes of			
			0–2,000 ft	2,001–4,000 ft	4,001–6,000 ft	6,001–8,000 ft
Hot	Pints	55 min	11 lb	12 lb	13 lb	14 lb
	Quarts	90	11	12	13	14

Pumpkins and Winter Squash

Recommended process time for Pumpkins and Winter Squash in a weighted-gauge pressure canner

Style of pack	Jar size	Process Time	Canner Pressure (PSI) at Altitudes of	
			0–1,000 ft	Above 1,000 ft
Hot	Pints	55 min	10 lb	15 lb
	Quarts	90	10	15

Soups

Vegetable, dried bean, or pea

Caution: Do not add noodles or other pasta, rice, flour, cream, milk, or other thickening agents to home-canned soups. If dried beans or peas are used, they must be fully rehydrated first.

Procedure: Select, wash, and prepare vegetables and/or dried beans or peas as described for the specific foods. Cook vegetables. For each cup of dried beans or peas, add 3 cups of water, boil 2 minutes, remove from heat, soak 1 hour, and heat to boil.

Drain all vegetables, beans, and/or peas and combine with meat broth, tomatoes, or water to cover. Boil 5 minutes. **Caution: Do not thicken.** Salt to taste, if desired.

Fill hot jars only halfway with mixture of solids. Add and cover with remaining liquid, leaving 1 inch of headspace. Remove air bubbles and adjust headspace if needed. Wipe rims of jars with a dampened, clean paper towel. Adjust lids, and process.

Soups

Recommended process time for Soups in a dial-gauge pressure canner

Style of pack	Jar size	Process Time	Canner Pressure (PSI) at Altitudes of			
			0–2,000 ft	2,001–4,000 ft	4,001–6,000 ft	6,001–8,000 ft
Hot	Pints	60 min	11 lb	12 lb	13 lb	14 lb
	Quarts	75	11	12	13	14

Soups

Recommended process time for Soups in a weighted-gauge pressure canner

Style of pack	Jar size	Process Time	Canner Pressure (PSI) at Altitudes of	
			0–1,000 ft	Above 1,000 ft
Hot	Pints	60 min	10 lb	15 lb
	Quarts	75	10	15

Spinach and Other Greens

Quantity: An average of 28 pounds is needed per canner load of 7 quarts; an average of 18 pounds is needed per canner load of 9 pints. A bushel weighs 18 pounds and yields 3 to 9 quarts—an average of 4 pounds per quart.

Quality: Can only freshly harvested greens. Discard any wilted, discolored, diseased, or insect-damaged leaves. Leaves should be tender and attractive in color.

Procedure: Wash only small amounts of greens at one time. Drain water and continue rinsing until water is clear and free of grit. Cut out tough stems and midribs. Place 1 pound of greens at a time in cheesecloth bag or blancher basket, and steam 3 to 5 minutes or until well wilted. Add ½ teaspoon of salt to each quart jar, if desired. Fill hot jars loosely with greens and add fresh boiling water, leaving 1 inch of headspace. Remove air bubbles and adjust headspace if needed. Wipe rims of jars with a dampened, clean paper towel. Adjust lids, and process.

Spinach and Other Greens

Recommended process time for Spinach and Other Greens in a dial-gauge pressure canner

Style of pack	Jar size	Process Time	Canner Pressure (PSI) at Altitudes of			
			0–2,000 ft	2,001–4,000 ft	4,001–6,000 ft	6,001–8,000 ft
Hot	Pints	70 min	11 lb	12 lb	13 lb	14 lb
	Quarts	90	11	12	13	14

Spinach and Other Greens

Recommended process time for Spinach and Other Greens in a weighted-gauge pressure canner

Style of pack	Jar size	Process Time	Canner Pressure (PSI) at Altitudes of	
			0–1,000 ft	Above 1,000 ft
Hot	Pints	70 min	10 lb	15 lb
	Quarts	90	10	15

Squash, Winter—Cubed

Prepare and process winter squash according to the instructions for "Pumpkin."

Succotash

15 lbs unhusked sweet corn or 3 qts cut whole kernels

14 lbs mature, green, podded lima beans or 4 quarts shelled limas

2 quarts crushed or whole tomatoes (optional)

YIELD: 7 quarts

Procedure: Wash and prepare fresh produce as described previously for specific vegetables. (For tomato preparation, see page 81 of accompanying guide *How to Prepare & Can Fruits, Jams, Jellies & More.*)

HOT PACK—Combine all prepared vegetables in a large kettle with enough water to cover the pieces. Add 1 teaspoon salt to each hot quart jar, if desired. Boil succotash gently for 5 minutes and fill hot jars with pieces and cooking liquid, leaving 1 inch of headspace.

RAW PACK—Fill hot jars with equal parts of all prepared vegetables, leaving 1 inch of headspace. Do not shake or press down pieces. Add 1 teaspoon salt to each quart jar, if desired. Add fresh boiling water, leaving 1 inch of headspace.

Remove air bubbles and adjust headspace if needed. Wipe rims of jars with a dampened, clean paper towel. Adjust lids, and process according to one of the tables below.

Succotash

Recommended process time for Succotash in a dial-gauge pressure canner

Style of pack	Jar size	Process Time	Canner Pressure (PSI) at Altitudes of			
			0–2,000 ft	2,001–4,000 ft	4,001–6,000 ft	6,001–8,000 ft
Hot or Raw	Pints	60 min	11 lb	12 lb	13 lb	14 lb
	Quarts	85	11	12	13	14

Succotash

Recommended process time for Succotash in a weighted-gauge pressure canner

Style of pack	Jar size	Process Time	Canner Pressure (PSI) at Altitudes of	
			0–1,000 ft	Above 1,000 ft
Hot or Raw	Pints	60 min	10 lb	15 lb
	Quarts	85	10	15

Chapter 3

Preparing and Canning Fermented Foods and Pickled Vegetables

Selection of fresh cucumbers

Quantity: An average of 14 pounds is needed per canner load of 7 quarts; an average of 9 pounds is needed per canner load of 9 pints. A bushel weighs 48 pounds and yields 16 to 24 quarts—an average of 2 pounds per quart.

Quality: Select firm cucumbers of the appropriate size: about 1½ inches long for gherkins and 4 inches long for dills. Use odd-shaped and more mature cucumbers for relishes and bread-and-butter-style pickles.

Low-temperature pasteurization treatment

The following treatment results in a better product texture but must be carefully managed to avoid possible spoilage. Place jars in a canner filled halfway with warm (120° to 140°F) water. Add hot water to 1 inch above jars. Heat water enough to maintain 180° to 185°F water temperature for 30 minutes. Use a candy or jelly thermometer to be sure water

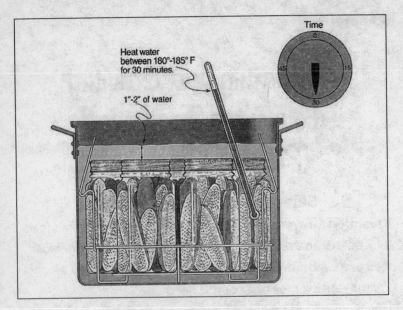

Heat water between 180°-185° F for 30 minutes.

1"-2" of water

Time

temperature is at least 180°F during entire 30 minutes. Temperatures higher than 185°F may cause unnecessary softening of pickles. **Caution: Use this pasteurization treatment only when recipe indicates.**

◊ ◈ ◊ ◈

Suitable containers, covers, and weights for fermenting food

A 1-gallon container is needed for each 5 pounds of fresh vegetables. Therefore, a 5-gallon stone crock is of ideal size for fermenting about 25 pounds of fresh cabbage or cucumbers. Food-grade plastic and glass containers are excellent substitutes for stone crocks. Other 1- to 3-gallon non-food-grade plastic containers may be used if lined inside with a clean, food-grade plastic bag. **Caution: Be certain that foods contact only food-grade plastics. Do not use garbage bags or trash liners.** Fermenting sauerkraut in quart and half-gallon Mason jars is an acceptable practice but may result in more spoilage losses.

Cabbage and cucumbers must be kept 1 to 2 inches under brine while fermenting. After adding prepared vegetables

and brine, insert a suitably sized dinner plate or glass pie plate inside the fermentation container. The plate must be slightly smaller than the container opening yet large enough to cover most of the shredded cabbage or cucumbers. To keep the plate under the brine, weight it down with 2 to 3 sealed quart jars filled with water. Covering the container opening with a clean, heavy bath towel helps to prevent contamination from insects and molds while the vegetables are fermenting. Fine-quality fermented vegetables are also obtained when the plate is weighted down with a very large, clean plastic bag filled with 3 quarts of water containing 4½ tablespoons of canning or pickling salt. Be sure to seal the plastic bag. Freezer bags sold for packaging turkeys are suitable for use with 5-gallon containers.

The fermentation container, plate, and jars must be washed in hot sudsy water and rinsed well with very hot water before use.

Salts used in pickling

Use of canning or pickling salt is recommended. Fermented and nonfermented pickles may be safely made using either iodized or noniodized table salt. However, noncaking materials added to table salts may make the brine cloudy. Flake salt varies in density and is not recommended for use.

Reduced-sodium salts—mixtures of sodium and potassium chloride, for example—may be used in quick pickle recipes, as indicated in this guide. The pickles may, however, have a slightly different taste than expected. **Caution: Use of reduced-sodium salt in fermented pickle recipes is not recommended.**

Fermented Foods

Dill Pickles

Use the following quantities for each gallon capacity of your container.

4 lbs of 4-inch-long pickling cucumbers
2 tbsp dill seed or 4 to 5 heads fresh or dry dill weed
½ cup salt
¼ cup vinegar (5%)
8 cups water and one or more of the following ingredients:
    2 cloves garlic (optional)
    2 dried red peppers (optional)
    2 tsp whole mixed pickling spices (optional)

Procedure: Wash cucumbers. Cut $1/16$ of an inch off blossom end and discard. Leave ¼ of an inch of stem attached. Place half of dill and spices on bottom of a clean, suitable container (see pages 84–86). Add cucumbers and remaining dill and spices. Dissolve salt in vinegar and water, and pour over cucumbers.

Add suitable cover and weight. Store where temperature is between 70° and 75°F for about 3 to 4 weeks while fermenting. Temperatures of 55° to 65°F are acceptable, but the fermentation will take 5 to 6 weeks. Avoid temperatures above 80°F, or pickles will become too soft during fermentation. Fermenting pickles cure slowly. Check the container several times a week and promptly remove surface scum or mold. **Caution: If the pickles become soft or slimy or develop a disagreeable odor, discard them.** Fully fermented pickles may be stored in the original container for about 4 to 6 months, provided they are refrigerated and surface scum and molds are removed regularly. Canning fully fermented pickles is a better way to store them. To can them, pour the brine into a pan, heat slowly to a boil, and simmer 5 minutes. Filter brine through paper coffee filters to reduce cloudiness, if desired. Fill hot jars with pickles and hot brine, leaving ½ of an inch of headspace. Remove air bubbles and adjust headspace if needed. Wipe rims of jars with a dampened, clean paper towel. Adjust lids, and process as specified in table below, or use the low-temperature pasteurization treatment described on pages 83–84.

Dill Pickles

Recommended process time for Dill Pickles in a boiling-water canner

Style of pack	Jar size	Process Time at Altitudes of		
		0–1,000 ft	1,001–6,000 ft	Above 6,000 ft
Raw	Pints	10 min	15	20
	Quarts	15	20	25

Sauerkraut

25 lbs cabbage
¾ cup canning or pickling salt

Quality: For the best sauerkraut, use firm heads of fresh cabbage. Shred cabbage and start kraut between 24 and 48 hours after harvest.

Yield: About 9 quarts

Procedure: Work with about 5 pounds of cabbage at a time. Discard outer leaves. Rinse heads under cold running water and drain. Cut heads in quarters and remove cores. Shred or slice to the thickness of a quarter. Put cabbage in a suitable fermentation container (see pages 84–86), and add 3 tablespoons salt. Mix thoroughly using clean hands. Pack firmly until salt draws juices from cabbage. Repeat shredding, salting, and packing until all cabbage is in the container. Be sure container is deep enough that its rim is at least 4 or 5 inches above the cabbage. If juice does not cover cabbage, add boiled and cooled brine (1½ tablespoons of salt per quart of water). Add plate and weights, and cover container with a clean bath towel. Store at 70° to 75°F while fermenting. At temperatures between 70° and 75°F, the kraut will be fully fermented in about 3 to 4 weeks; at 60° to 65°F, fermentation may take 5 to 6 weeks. At temperatures lower than 60°F, the kraut may not ferment. Above 75°F, the kraut may become soft.

If you weigh the cabbage down with a brine-filled bag, do not disturb the crock until normal fermentation is completed (when bubbling ceases). If you use jars as weight, you will have to check the kraut 2 to 3 times each week and remove any scum that may form. Fully fermented kraut may be kept tightly covered in the refrigerator for several months, or it may be canned as follows:

HOT PACK—Bring kraut and liquid slowly to a boil in a large kettle, stirring frequently. Remove from heat and fill hot jars rather firmly with hot kraut and juices, leaving ½ of an inch of headspace.

RAW PACK—Fill hot jars firmly with raw kraut, and cover kraut with juices, leaving ½ of an inch of headspace.

Remove air bubbles and adjust headspace if needed. Wipe rims of jars with a dampened, clean paper towel. Adjust lids, and process.

Sauerkraut

Recommended process time for Sauerkraut in a boiling-water canner

Style of pack	Jar size	Process Time at Altitudes of			
		0–1,000 ft	1,001–3,000 ft	3,001–6,000 ft	Above 6,000 ft
Hot	Pints	10 min	15	15	20
	Quarts	15	20	20	25
Raw	Pints	20	25	30	35
	Quarts	25	30	35	40

Cucumber Pickles
Bread-and-Butter Pickles

6 lbs of 4- to 5-inch-long pickling cucumbers

8 cups thinly sliced onions (about 3 pounds)

½ cup canning or pickling salt

4 cups vinegar (5%)

4½ cups sugar

2 tbsp mustard seed

1½ tbsp celery seed

1 tbsp ground turmeric

1 cup pickling lime (optional) for use in variation below for
   making firmer pickles

Yield: About 8 pints

Procedure: Wash cucumbers. Cut ¹⁄₁₆ of an inch off blossom end and discard. Cut cucumber into ³⁄₁₆-inch slices. Combine cucumbers and onions in a large bowl. Add salt. Cover with 2 inches crushed or cubed ice. Refrigerate 3 to 4 hours, adding more ice as needed.

Combine remaining ingredients in a large pot. Boil 10 minutes. Drain cucumbers and onions, add to pot, and slowly reheat ingredients to boiling. Fill hot pint jars with hot slices and cooking syrup, leaving ½ of an inch of headspace. Remove air bubbles and adjust headspace if needed. Wipe rims of jars with a dampened, clean paper towel. Adjust lids, and process as specified in the table on the next page, or use the low-temperature pasteurization treatment from pages 83–84.

Variation for firmer pickles: After washing and slicing cucumbers but before continuing with the rest of the procedure described on the previous page, mix 1 cup pickling lime and ½ cup salt with 1 gallon water in a 2- to 3-gallon crock or enamelware container. **Caution: Avoid inhaling lime dust while mixing the lime-water solution.** Soak cucumber slices in lime water for 12 to 24 hours, stirring occasionally. Remove from lime solution, rinse, and resoak 1 hour in fresh cold water. Repeat the rinsing and soaking steps 2 more times. Handle carefully, as slices will be brittle. Drain well.

Storage: After processing and cooling, jars should be stored at least 4 to 5 weeks to develop ideal flavor.

Variation: Substitute slender (1 to 1½ inches in diameter) zucchini or yellow summer squash for cucumbers.

Bread-and-Butter Pickles

Recommended process time for Bread-and-Butter Pickles in a boiling-water canner

Style of pack	Jar size	Process Time at Altitudes of		
		0–1,000 ft	1,001–6,000 ft	Above 6,000 ft
Hot	Pints or Quarts	10 min	15	20

Quick Fresh-Pack Dill Pickles

8 lbs of 3- to 5-inch-long pickling cucumbers

2 gallons water

1¼ cups canning or pickling salt (divided)

1½ quarts vinegar (5%)

¼ cup sugar

2 quarts water

2 tbsp whole mixed pickling spice

about 3 tbsp whole mustard seed (1 tsp per pint jar)

about 14 heads of fresh dill (1½ heads per pint jar) or 4½ tbsp
dill seed (1½ tsp per pint jar)

Yield: About 7 to 9 pints

Procedure: Wash cucumbers. Cut ¹⁄₁₆ of an inch off blossom end and discard, but leave ¼ of an inch of stem attached. Dissolve ¾ cup salt in 2 gallons water. Pour over cucumbers and let stand 12 hours. Drain. Combine vinegar, ½ cup salt, sugar, and 2 quarts water. Add mixed pickling spice tied in a clean white cloth. Heat to boiling. Fill hot jars with cucumbers. Add 1 teaspoon mustard seed and 1½ heads fresh dill per pint. Cover with boiling pickling solution, leaving ½ of an inch of headspace. Remove air bubbles and adjust headspace if needed. Wipe rims of jars with a dampened, clean paper towel. Adjust lids, and process as specified in table below, or use the low-temperature pasteurization treatment (pages 83–84).

Quick Fresh-Pack Dill Pickles

Recommended process time for Fresh-Pack Dill Pickles in a boiling-water canner

Style of pack	Jar size	Process Time at Altitudes of		
		0-1,000 ft	1,001-6,000 ft	Above 6,000 ft
Raw	Pints	10 min	15	20
	Quarts	15	20	25

Sweet Gherkin Pickles

7 lbs cucumbers (1½ inches long or less)

½ cup canning or pickling salt

6 cups vinegar (5%)

8 cups sugar

¾ tsp turmeric

2 tsp celery seeds

2 tsp whole mixed pickling spice

2 cinnamon sticks

½ tsp fennel (optional)

2 tsp vanilla (optional)

Yield: About 6 to 7 pints

Procedure: Wash cucumbers. Cut ¹⁄₁₆ of an inch off blossom end and discard, but leave ¼ of an inch of stem attached. Place cucumbers in large container and cover with boiling water. Six to eight hours later, and again **on the second day,** drain and cover with 6 quarts of fresh boiling water containing ¼ cup salt. **On the third day,** drain and prick cucumbers with a table fork. Combine and bring to a boil 3 cups vinegar, 3 cups sugar, turmeric, and spices. Pour over cucumbers. Six to eight hours later, drain and save pickling syrup. Add another 2 cups each of sugar and vinegar and reheat to a boil. Pour over pickles. **On the fourth day,** drain and save syrup. Add another 2 cups sugar and 1 cup vinegar. Heat to boiling and pour over pickles. Six to eight hours later, drain and save pickling syrup. Add 1 cup sugar and 2 teaspoons vanilla and heat to boiling. Fill hot, sterile pint jars (see page 26) with pickles and cover with hot syrup, leaving ½ of an inch of headspace. Remove air bubbles and adjust headspace if needed. Wipe rims of jars with a dampened, clean paper towel. Adjust lids, and process as specified in table below, or use the low-temperature pasteurization treatment (pages 83–84).

Sweet Gherkin Pickles

Recommended process time for Sweet Gherkin Pickles in a boiling-water canner

Style of pack	Jar size	Process Time at Altitudes of		
		0–1,000 ft	1,001–6,000 ft	Above 6,000 ft
Raw	Pints	5 min	10	15

14-Day Sweet Pickles

Can be canned whole, in strips, or in slices

4 lbs of 2- to 5-inch-long pickling cucumbers (If packed whole, use cucumbers of uniform size.)

¾ cup canning or pickling salt (separated into ¼ cups to be added on the 1st, 3rd, and 5th days)

2 tsp celery seed

2 tbsp mixed pickling spices

5½ cups sugar

4 cups vinegar (5%)

Yield: About 5 to 9 pints

Procedure: Wash cucumbers. Cut ¹⁄₁₆ of an inch off blossom end and discard, but leave ¼ of an inch of stem attached. Place whole cucumbers in a suitable 1-gallon container (see pages 84–86). Add ¼ cup canning or pickling salt to 2 quarts water, and bring to a boil. Pour over cucumbers. Add suitable cover and weight. Place clean towel over container and keep the temperature at about 70°F. **On the third and fifth days,** drain salt water and discard. Rinse cucumbers, and rescald (rinse well with very hot water) the cover and weight. Return cucumbers to container. Add ¼ cup salt to 2 quarts fresh water, and boil. Pour over cucumbers. Replace cover and weight, and re-cover with clean towel. **On the seventh day,** drain salt water and discard. Rinse cucumbers and rescald containers, cover, and weight. Slice or strip cucumbers, if desired, and return to container. Place celery seed and pickling spices in small cheese-cloth bag. Combine 2 cups sugar and 4 cups vinegar in a saucepan. Add spice bag, bring to a boil, and pour pickling solution over cucumbers. Add cover and weight, and re-cover with clean towel. **On each of the next six days,** drain syrup and spice bag and save. Add ½ cup sugar to syrup and bring to a boil in a saucepan each day. Remove cucumbers and rinse. Scald container, cover, and weight daily. Return cucumbers to container; add boiled syrup, cover, and weight; and re-cover with towel. **On the 14th day,** drain syrup into saucepan. Fill hot, sterile pint jars (see page 26) or clean, hot quart jars with cucumbers, leaving ½ of an inch of headspace. Add ½ cup sugar to syrup and bring to a boil. Remove spice bag. Pour hot syrup over cucumbers, leaving ½ of an inch of headspace. Remove air bubbles and adjust headspace if needed. Wipe rims of jars with a dampened, clean paper towel. Adjust lids, and process as specified in table on next page, or use the low-temperature pasteurization treatment from pages 83–84.

14-Day Sweet Pickles

Recommended process time for 14-Day Sweet Pickles in a boiling-water canner

Style of pack	Jar size	Process Time at Altitudes of		
		0–1,000 ft	1,001–6,000 ft	Above 6,000 ft
Raw	Pints	5 min	10	15
	Quarts	10	15	20

Quick Sweet Pickles

May be canned as either strips or slices

8 lbs of 3- to 4-inch-long pickling cucumbers

⅓ cup canning or pickling salt

4½ cups sugar

3½ cups vinegar (5%)

2 tsp celery seed

1 tbsp whole allspice

2 tbsp mustard seed

1 cup pickling lime (optional) for use in variation on next page for making firmer pickles

Yield: About 7 to 9 pints

Procedure: Wash cucumbers. Cut ¹⁄₁₆ of an inch off blossom end and discard, but leave ¼ of an inch of stem attached. Slice or cut in strips. Place in bowl and sprinkle with ⅓ cup salt. Cover with 2 inches of crushed or cubed ice. Refrigerate 3 to 4 hours. Add more ice as needed. Drain well.

Combine sugar, vinegar, celery seed, allspice, and mustard seed in 6-quart kettle. Heat to boiling.

HOT PACK—Add cucumbers, and heat slowly until vinegar solution returns to boil. Stir occasionally to make sure mixture heats evenly. Fill sterile jars, leaving ½ of an inch of headspace.

RAW PACK—Fill hot jars, leaving ½ of an inch of headspace. Add hot pickling syrup, leaving ½ of an inch of headspace.

Remove air bubbles and adjust headspace if needed. Wipe rims of jars with a dampened, clean paper towel. Adjust lids, and process according to the table on the top of the next page, or use the low-temperature pasteurization treatment described on pages 83–84.

Variation for firmer pickles: After washing and slicing cucumbers but before continuing with the rest of the procedure described on the previous page, mix 1 cup pickling lime and ½ cup salt with 1 gallon water in a 2- to 3-gallon crock or enamelware container. **Caution: Avoid inhaling lime dust while mixing the lime-water solution.** Soak cucumber slices or strips in lime-water solution for 12 to 24 hours, stirring occasionally. Remove from lime solution, rinse, and resoak 1 hour in fresh cold water. Repeat the rinsing and resoaking 2 more times. Handle carefully because slices or strips will be brittle. Drain well.

Quick Sweet Pickles

Recommended process time for Quick Sweet Pickles in a boiling-water canner

Style of pack	Jar size	Process Time at Altitudes of		
		0–1,000 ft	1,001–6,000 ft	Above 6,000 ft
Hot	Pints or Quarts	5 min	10	15
Raw	Pints	10	15	20
	Quarts	15	20	25

Storage: After processing and cooling, jars should be stored at least 4 to 5 weeks to develop ideal flavor.

Variation: Add 2 slices of raw whole onion to each jar before filling with cucumbers.

Other Vegetable Pickles

Pickled Asparagus

Yield: 6 wide-mouth pint jars

10 lbs asparagus

6 large garlic cloves

4½ cups water

4½ cups white distilled vinegar (5%)

6 small hot peppers (optional)

½ cup canning salt

3 tsp dill seed

Yield: 7 twelve-ounce jars

7 lbs asparagus

7 large garlic cloves

3 cups water

3 cups white distilled vinegar (5%)

7 small hot peppers (optional)

⅓ cup canning salt

2 tsp dill seed

Procedure: Wash asparagus well, but gently, under running water. Cut stems from the bottom to leave spears with tips that fit into the canning jar, leaving a little more than ½ of an inch of headspace. Peel and wash garlic cloves. Place a garlic clove at the bottom of each jar, and tightly pack asparagus into hot jars with the blunt ends down. In an 8-quart saucepot, combine water, vinegar, hot peppers (optional), salt, and dill seed. Bring to a boil. Place a hot pepper (if used) over asparagus spears in each jar. Pour boiling-hot pickling brine over spears, leaving ½ of an inch of headspace. Remove air bubbles and adjust headspace if needed. Wipe rims of jars with a dampened, clean paper towel. Adjust lids, and process.

Pickled Asparagus

Recommended process time for Pickled Asparagus in a boiling-water canner

Style of pack	Jar size	Process Time at Altitudes of		
		0–1,000 ft	1,001–6,000 ft	Above 6,000 ft
Raw	12-ounce or Pints	10 min	15	20

Pickled Dilled Beans

4 lbs fresh, tender green or yellow beans (5 to 6 inches long)

8 to 16 heads fresh dill

8 cloves garlic (optional)

½ cup canning or pickling salt

4 cups white vinegar (5%)

4 cups water

1 tsp hot red pepper flakes (optional)

Yield: About 8 pints

Procedure: Wash beans, trim ends, and cut to 4-inch lengths. In each hot sterile pint jar (see page 26), place 1 to 2 dill heads and, if desired, 1 clove of garlic. Place whole beans upright in jars, leaving ½ of an inch of headspace. Trim beans to ensure proper fit, if necessary. Combine salt, vinegar, water, and pepper flakes (if desired). Bring to a boil. Add hot solution to beans, leaving ½ of an inch of headspace. Remove air bubbles and adjust headspace if needed. Wipe rims of jars with a dampened, clean paper towel. Adjust lids, and process.

Pickled Dilled Beans

Recommended process time for Pickled Dilled Beans in a boiling-water canner

Style of pack	Jar size	Process Time at Altitudes of		
		0–1,000 ft	1,001–6,000 ft	Above 6,000 ft
Raw	Pints	5 min	10	15

Pickled Three-Bean Salad

1½ cups cut and blanched green or yellow beans (prepared as described on next page)

1½ cups canned, drained red kidney beans

1 cup canned, drained garbanzo beans

½ cup peeled and thinly sliced onion (about 1 medium onion)

½ cup trimmed and thinly sliced celery (1½ medium stalks)

½ cup sliced green peppers (½ medium pepper)

½ cup white vinegar (5%)

¼ cup bottled lemon juice

¾ cup sugar

1¼ cups water

¼ cup oil

½ tsp canning or pickling salt

Yield: About 5 to 6 half-pints

Procedure: Wash fresh beans, and snap off ends. Cut or snap into 1- to 2-inch pieces. Blanch 3 minutes and cool immediately. Rinse kidney beans with tap water and drain again. Prepare and measure all other vegetables. Combine vinegar, lemon juice, sugar, and water and bring to a boil. Remove from heat. Add oil and salt and mix well. Add beans, onions, celery, and green pepper to solution and bring to a simmer. Remove from heat, marinate 12 to 14 hours in refrigerator, then heat entire mixture to a boil. Fill hot jars with hot solids. Add hot liquid, leaving ½ of an inch of headspace. Remove air bubbles and adjust headspace if needed. Wipe rims of jars with a dampened, clean paper towel. Adjust lids, and process.

Pickled Three-Bean Salad

Recommended process time for Pickled Three-Bean Salad in a boiling-water canner

Style of pack	Jar size	Process Time at Altitudes of		
		0–1,000 ft	1,001–6,000 ft	Above 6,000 ft
Hot	Half-pints or Pints	15 min	20	25

Pickled Beets

7 lbs of 2- to 2½-inch-diameter beets

4 cups vinegar (5%)

1½ tsp canning or pickling salt

2 cups sugar

2 cups water

2 cinnamon sticks

12 whole cloves

4 to 6 onions (2- to 2½-inch diameter), if desired

Yield: About 8 pints

Procedure: Trim off beet tops, leaving 1 inch of stem and roots to prevent bleeding of color. Wash thoroughly. Sort for size. Cover similar-size beets with boiling water and cook until tender (about 25 to 30 minutes). **Caution: Drain and discard liquid.** Cool beets. Trim off roots and stems, and slip off skins. Slice into ¼-inch slices. Peel and thinly slice onions. Combine vinegar, salt, sugar, and fresh water. Put spices in cheesecloth bag and add to vinegar mixture. Bring to a boil. Add beets and onions. Simmer 5 minutes. Remove spice bag. Fill hot jars with beets and onions, leaving ½ of an inch of headspace. Add hot vinegar solution, allowing ½ of an inch of headspace. Remove air bubbles and adjust headspace if needed. Wipe rims of jars with a dampened, clean paper towel. Adjust lids, and process.

Variation: For pickled whole baby beets, follow above directions but use beets that are 1 to 1½ inches in diameter. Pack whole; do not slice. Onions may be omitted.

Pickled Beets

Recommended process time for Pickled Beets in a boiling-water canner

Style of pack	Jar size	Process Time at Altitudes of			
		0–1,000 ft	1,001–3,000 ft	3,001–6,000 ft	Above 6,000 ft
Hot	Pints or Quarts	30 min	35	40	45

Pickled Carrots

2¾ lbs peeled carrots (about 3½ lbs as purchased)

5½ cups white vinegar (5%)

1 cup water

2 cups sugar

2 tsp canning salt

8 tsp mustard seed

4 tsp celery seed

Yield: About 4 pints

Procedure: Wash and peel carrots. Cut into rounds that are approximately ½ inch thick. Combine vinegar, water, sugar, and canning salt in an 8-quart Dutch oven or stockpot. Bring to a boil and boil 3 minutes. Add carrots and bring back to a boil. Then reduce heat to a simmer and heat until half-cooked (about 10 minutes). Meanwhile, place 2 teaspoons mustard seed and 1 teaspoon celery seed into each empty, hot pint jar. Fill jars with hot carrots, leaving 1 inch of headspace. Fill with hot pickling liquid, leaving ½ of an inch of headspace. Remove air bubbles and adjust headspace if needed. Wipe rims of jars with a dampened, clean paper towel. Adjust lids, and process.

Pickled Carrots

Recommended process time for Pickled Carrots in a boiling-water canner

Style of pack	Jar size	Process Time at Altitudes of		
		0–1,000 ft	1,001–6,000 ft	Above 6,000 ft
Hot	Pints	15 min	20	25

Pickled Baby Carrots

Procedure: Follow the directions and process time for Pickled Carrots, using 8½ cups peeled baby carrots but leaving the carrots whole.

Pickled Cauliflower or Brussels Sprouts

12 cups of 1- to 2-inch-diameter cauliflower flowerets or small brussels sprouts

4 cups white vinegar (5%)

2 cups sugar

2 cups thinly sliced onions

1 cup diced sweet red peppers

2 tbsp mustard seed

1 tbsp celery seed

1 tsp turmeric

1 tsp hot red pepper flakes

Yield: About 9 half-pints

Procedure: Wash cauliflower flowerets or brussels sprouts (remove stems and blemished outer leaves from sprouts) and boil in salt water (4 teaspoons canning salt per gallon of water) for 3 minutes for cauliflower and 4 minutes for brussels sprouts. Drain and cool. Combine vinegar, sugar, onion, diced red pepper, and spices in large saucepan. Bring to a boil and simmer 5 minutes. Distribute onion and diced pepper among jars. Fill hot jars with flowerets or sprouts and hot pickling solution, leaving ½ of an inch of headspace. Remove air bubbles and adjust head-space if needed. Wipe rims of jars with a dampened, clean paper towel. Adjust lids, and process.

Pickled Cauliflower or Brussels Sprouts

Recommended process time for Pickled Cauliflower or Brussels Sprouts in a boiling-water canner

Style of pack	Jar size	Process Time at Altitudes of		
		0-1,000 ft	1,001-6,000 ft	Above 6,000 ft
Hot	Half-pints or Pints	10 min	15	20

Chayote and Jicama Slaw

4 cups julienned jicama

4 cups julienned chayote

2 cups finely chopped red bell pepper

2 finely chopped hot peppers

2½ cups water

2½ cups cider vinegar (5%)

½ cup white sugar

3½ tsp canning salt

1 tsp celery seed (optional)

Yield: About 6 half-pints

Procedure: Caution: Wear plastic or rubber gloves and do not touch your face while handling or cutting hot peppers. If you do not wear gloves, wash hands thoroughly with soap and water before touching your face or eyes. Wash, peel, and thinly julienne jicama and chayote, discarding the seed of the chayote. In an 8-quart Dutch oven or stockpot, combine all ingredients except chayote. Bring to a boil and boil for 5 minutes. Reduce heat to simmering and add chayote. Bring back to a boil and then turn heat off. Fill hot half-pint jars with hot solids, leaving ½ of an inch of headspace. Cover with boiling cooking liquid, leaving ½ of an inch of headspace. Remove air bubbles and adjust headspace if needed. Wipe rims of jars with a dampened, clean paper towel. Adjust lids, and process.

Chayote and Jicama Slaw

Recommended process time for Chayote and Jicama Slaw in a boiling-water canner

Style of pack	Jar size	Process Time at Altitudes of		
		0--1,000 ft	1,001–6,000 ft	Above 6,000 ft
Hot	Half-pints	15 min	20	25

Bread-and-Butter Pickled Jicama

14 cups cubed jicama

3 cups thinly sliced onion

1 cup chopped red bell pepper

4 cups white vinegar (5%)

4½ cups sugar

2 tbsp mustard seed

1 tbsp celery seed

1 tsp ground turmeric

Yield: About 6 pints

Procedure: Combine vinegar, sugar, and spices in a 12-quart Dutch oven or large saucepot. Stir and bring to a boil. Stir in jicama cubes, onion slices, and red bell pepper. Return to a boil, reduce heat, and simmer 5 minutes. Stir occasionally. Fill hot pint jars with hot solids, leaving ½ of an inch of headspace. Cover with boiling cooking liquid, leaving ½ of an inch of headspace. Remove air bubbles and adjust headspace if needed. Wipe rims of jars with a dampened, clean paper towel. Adjust lids, and process.

Bread-and-Butter Pickled Jicama

Recommended process time for Bread-and-Butter Pickled Jicama in a boiling-water canner

Style of pack	Jar size	Process Time at Altitudes of		
		0–1,000 ft	1,001–6,000 ft	Above 6,000 ft
Hot	Pints	15 min	20	25

Marinated Whole Mushrooms

7 lbs small whole mushrooms
½ cup bottled lemon juice
2 cups olive or salad oil
2½ cups white vinegar (5%)
1 tbsp oregano leaves
1 tbsp dried basil leaves
1 tbsp canning or pickling salt
½ cup finely chopped onions
½ cup diced pimiento
2 cloves garlic, cut in quarters
25 black peppercorns

Yield: About 9 half-pints

Procedure: Select very fresh, unopened mushrooms with caps less than 1¼ inches in diameter. Wash. Cut stems, leaving ¼ of an inch attached to cap. Put mushrooms in a pot, and add lemon juice and water to cover. Bring to a boil. Simmer 5 minutes. Drain mushrooms, and reserve. Mix olive oil, vinegar, oregano, basil, and salt in a saucepan. Stir in onions and pimiento and heat to boiling. Place ¼ garlic clove and 2 to 3 peppercorns in each half-pint jar. Fill hot jars with mushrooms and hot, well-mixed oil/vinegar solution, leaving ½ of an inch of headspace. Remove air bubbles and adjust headspace if needed. Wipe rims of jars with a dampened, clean paper towel. Adjust lids, and process according to the table at the top of the next page.

Marinated Whole Mushrooms

Recommended process time for Marinated Whole Mushrooms in a boiling-water canner

Style of pack	Jar size	Process Time at Altitudes of			
		0–1,000 ft	1,001–3,000 ft	3,001–6,000 ft	Above 6,000 ft
Hot	Half-pints	20 min	25	30	35

Pickled Dilled Okra

7 lbs small okra pods

6 small hot peppers

4 tsp dill seed

8 to 9 garlic cloves

⅔ cup canning or pickling salt

6 cups water

6 cups vinegar (5%)

Yield: About 8 to 9 pints

Procedure: Wash and trim okra. Fill hot jars firmly with whole okra, leaving ½ of an inch of headspace. Place 1 garlic clove in each jar. Combine salt, hot peppers, dill seed, water, and vinegar in large saucepan and bring to a boil. Pour hot pickling solution over okra, leaving ½ of an inch of headspace. Remove air bubbles and adjust headspace if needed. Wipe rims of jars with a dampened, clean paper towel. Adjust lids, and process according to the table at the top of the next page.

Pickled Dilled Okra

Recommended process time for Pickled Dilled Okra in a boiling-water canner

Style of pack	Jar size	Process Time at Altitudes of		
		0–1,000 ft	1,001–6,000 ft	Above 6,000 ft
Hot	Pints	10 min	15	20

Pickled Pearl Onions

8 cups peeled, white pearl onions

5½ cups white vinegar (5%)

1 cup water

2 tsp canning salt

2 cups sugar

8 tsp mustard seed

4 tsp celery seed

Yield: About 3 to 4 pints

Procedure: To peel onions, place a few at a time in a wire-mesh basket or strainer, dip in boiling water for 30 seconds, then remove and place in cold water for 30 seconds. Cut a ¹⁄₁₆-inch slice from the root end, and then remove the peel and cut ¹⁄₁₆ of an inch from the other end of the onion. Combine vinegar, water, salt, and sugar in an 8-quart Dutch oven or stockpot. Bring to a boil and boil 3 minutes. Add peeled onions and bring back to a boil. Reduce heat to a simmer and heat until half-cooked (about 5 minutes). Meanwhile, place 2 teaspoons mustard seed and 1 teaspoon celery seed into each empty, hot pint jar. Fill with hot onions, leaving 1 inch of headspace. Fill with hot pickling liquid, leaving ½ of an inch of headspace. Remove air bubbles and adjust headspace if needed. Wipe rims of jars with a dampened, clean paper towel. Adjust lids, and process.

Pickled Pearl Onions

Recommended process time for Pickled Pearl Onions in a boiling-water canner

Style of pack	Jar size	Process Time at Altitudes of		
		0–1,000 ft	1,001–6,000 ft	Above 6,000 ft
Hot	Pints	10 min	15	20

Marinated Peppers

Bell, Hungarian, banana, or jalapeño

4 lbs firm peppers*

1 cup bottled lemon juice

2 cups white vinegar (5%)

1 tbsp oregano leaves

1 cup olive or salad oil

½ cup chopped onions

2¼ tsp canning or pickling salt

2 cloves garlic, quartered (optional)

2 tbsp prepared horseradish (optional)

*Note: It is possible to adjust the intensity of pickled jalapeño peppers by using all hot jalapeño peppers (hot style) or by mixing in sweet and mild peppers (medium or mild style):

FOR HOT STYLE: Use 4 pounds jalapeño peppers.

FOR MEDIUM STYLE: Use 2 pounds jalapeño peppers and 2 pounds sweet and mild peppers.

FOR MILD STYLE: Use 1 pound jalapeño peppers and 3 pounds sweet and mild peppers.

Yield: About 9 half-pints

Procedure: Select your favorite pepper. **Caution: If you select hot peppers, wear plastic or rubber gloves and do not touch your face while handling or cutting hot peppers. If you do not wear gloves, wash hands thoroughly with soap and water before touching your face or eyes.** Peppers may be left whole. Large peppers may be quartered. Wash, slash 2 to 4 slits in each pepper, and blanch in boiling water or, for tough-skinned hot peppers, blister skins using one of these two methods:

Oven or broiler method to blister skins—Place peppers in a hot oven (400°F) or under a broiler for 6 to 8 minutes until skins blister.

Range-top method to blister skins—Cover hot burner (either gas or electric) with heavy wire mesh. Place peppers on mesh-covered burner for several minutes until skins blister.

After blistering skins, place peppers in a pan and cover with a damp cloth. (This will make peeling the peppers easier.) Cool several minutes; peel off skins. Flatten whole peppers. Mix remaining ingredients except salt and garlic in a saucepan, and heat to boiling. Place ¼ garlic clove (optional) and ¼ teaspoon salt in each hot half-pint jar. Fill hot jars with peppers. Pour hot, well-mixed oil/pickling solution over peppers, leaving ½ of an inch of headspace. Remove air bubbles and adjust headspace if needed. Wipe rims of jars with a dampened, clean paper towel. Adjust lids, and process.

Marinated Peppers

Recommended process time for Marinated Peppers in a boiling-water canner

Style of pack	Jar size	Process Time at Altitudes of		
		0–1,000 ft	1,001–6,000 ft	Above 6,000 ft
Raw	Half-pints or Pints	15 min	20	25

Pickled Bell Peppers

7 lbs firm bell peppers

3½ cups sugar

3 cups vinegar (5%)

3 cups water

9 cloves garlic

4½ tsp canning or pickling salt

Yield: About 9 pints

Procedure: Wash peppers, cut into quarters, remove cores and seeds, and cut away any blemishes. Slice peppers into strips. Boil sugar, vinegar, and water for 1 minute. Add peppers and bring to a boil. Place ½ clove of garlic and ¼ teaspoon salt in each hot, sterile (see page 26) half-pint jar; double the amounts for pint jars. Add pepper strips, and cover with hot vinegar mixture, leaving ½ of an inch of headspace. Remove air bubbles and adjust headspace if needed. Wipe rims of jars with a dampened, clean paper towel. Adjust lids, and process.

Pickled Bell Peppers

Recommended process time for Pickled Bell Peppers in a boiling-water canner

Style of pack	Jar size	Process Time at Altitudes of		
		0–1,000 ft	1,001–6,000 ft	Above 6,000 ft
Hot	Half-pints or Pints	5 min	10	15

Pickled Hot Peppers

Hungarian, banana, chile, jalapeño

4 lbs hot long peppers (red, green, or yellow)

3 lbs sweet red and green peppers, mixed

5 cups vinegar (5%)

1 cup water

4 tsp canning or pickling salt

2 tbsp sugar

2 cloves garlic

Yield: About 9 pints

Procedure: Caution: Wear plastic or rubber gloves and do not touch your face while handling or cutting hot peppers. If you do not wear gloves, wash hands thoroughly with soap and water before touching your face or eyes. Wash peppers. If small peppers are left whole, slash 2 to 4 slits in each. Cut large peppers into quarters. Blanch peppers in boiling water or, for tough-skinned hot peppers, blister skins using one of these two methods:

Oven or broiler method to blister skins—Place peppers in a hot oven (400°F) or under a broiler for 6 to 8 minutes until skins blister.

Range-top method to blister skins—Cover hot burner (either gas or electric) with heavy wire mesh. Place peppers on mesh-covered burner for several minutes until skins blister.

After blistering skins, place peppers in a pan and cover with a damp cloth. (This will make peeling the peppers easier.) Cool several minutes; peel off skins. Flatten small peppers. Cut large peppers into quarters. Fill hot jars with peppers, leaving ½ of an inch of headspace. Combine other ingredients, heat to boiling, and simmer 10 minutes. Remove garlic. Add hot pickling solution to cover peppers, leaving ½ of an inch of headspace. Remove air bubbles and adjust headspace if needed. Wipe rims of jars with a dampened, clean paper towel. Adjust lids, and process.

Pickled Hot Peppers

Recommended process time for Pickled Hot Peppers in a boiling-water canner

Style of pack	Jar size	Process Time at Altitudes of		
		0–1,000 ft	1,001–6,000 ft	Above 6,000 ft
Raw	Half-pints or Pints	10 min	15	20

Pickled Jalapeño Pepper Rings

3 lbs jalapeño peppers

1½ cups pickling lime

1½ gallons water

7½ cups cider vinegar (5%)

1¾ cups water

2½ tbsp canning salt

3 tbsp celery seed

6 tbsp mustard seed

Yield: About 6 pint jars

Procedure: Caution: Wear plastic or rubber gloves and do not touch your face while handling or cutting hot peppers. If you do not wear gloves, wash hands thoroughly with soap and water before touching your face or eyes. Wash peppers well and slice into ¼-inch-thick slices. Discard stem end. Mix 1½ cups pickling lime with 1½ gallons water in a stainless steel, glass, or food-grade plastic container. **Avoid inhaling lime dust while mixing lime-water solution.** Soak pepper slices in lime water in the refrigerator for 18 hours, stirring occasionally (12 to 24 hours may be used). Drain lime solution from soaked pepper rings. Rinse peppers gently but thoroughly with water. Cover pepper rings with fresh cold water and soak in the refrigerator 1 hour. Drain water from peppers. Repeat the rinsing, soaking, and draining steps two more times. Drain thoroughly at the end. Place 1 tablespoon mustard seed and 1½ teaspoons celery seed in the bottom of each hot pint jar. Pack drained pepper rings into the jars, leaving ½ of an inch of headspace. Bring cider vinegar, 1¾ cups water, and canning salt to a boil over high heat. Ladle boiling-hot brine solution over pepper rings in jars, leaving ½ of an inch of headspace. Remove air bubbles and adjust headspace if needed. Wipe rims of jars with a dampened, clean paper towel. Adjust lids, and process.

Pickled Jalapeño Pepper Rings

Recommended process time for Pickled Jalapeño Pepper Rings in a boiling-water canner

Style of pack	Jar size	Process Time at Altitudes of		
		0– 1,000 ft	1,001– 6,000 ft	Above 6,000 ft
Hot	Pints	10 min	15	20

Pickled Yellow Pepper Rings

2½ to 3 lbs yellow (banana) peppers

2 tbsp celery seed

4 tbsp mustard seed

5 cups cider vinegar (5%)

1¼ cups water

5 tsp canning salt

Yield: About 4 pint jars

Procedure: Caution: Wear plastic or rubber gloves and do not touch your face while handling or cutting hot peppers. If you do not wear gloves, wash hands thoroughly with soap and water before touching your face or eyes. Wash peppers well and remove stem end of each; slice peppers into

¼-inch-thick rings. Place ½ tablespoon celery seed and 1 tablespoon mustard seed in bottom of each empty, hot pint jar. Fill jars with pepper rings, leaving ½ of an inch of headspace. In a 4-quart Dutch oven or saucepan, combine the cider vinegar, water, and salt; heat to boiling. Cover pepper rings with boiling liquid, leaving ½ of an inch of headspace. Remove air bubbles and adjust headspace if needed. Wipe rims of jars with a dampened, clean paper towel. Adjust lids, and process.

Pickled Yellow Pepper Rings

Recommended process time for Pickled Yellow Pepper Rings in a boiling-water canner

Style of pack	Jar size	Process Time at Altitudes of		
		0–1,000 ft	1,001–6,000 ft	Above 6,000 ft
Hot	Pints	10 min	15	20

Pickled Sweet Green Tomatoes

10 to 11 lbs of green tomatoes (16 cups sliced)

2 cups sliced onions

¼ cup canning or pickling salt

3 cups brown sugar

4 cups vinegar (5%)

1 tbsp mustard seed

1 tbsp allspice

1 tbsp celery seed

1 tbsp whole cloves

Yield: About 9 pints

Procedure: Wash and slice tomatoes and onions. Place in bowl, sprinkle with ¼ cup salt, and let stand 4 to 6 hours. Drain. Heat and stir sugar in vinegar until dissolved. Tie mustard seed, allspice, celery seed, and cloves in a spice bag. Add to vinegar along with tomatoes and onions. If needed, add minimum water to cover pieces. Bring to a boil and simmer 30 minutes, stirring as needed to prevent burning. Tomatoes should be tender and transparent when properly cooked. Remove spice bag. Fill hot jars with solids, and cover with hot pickling solution, leaving ½ of an inch of headspace. Remove air bubbles and adjust headspace if needed. Wipe rims of jars with a dampened, clean paper towel. Adjust lids, and process.

Pickled Sweet Green Tomatoes

Recommended process time for Pickled Sweet Green Tomatoes in a boiling-water canner

Style of pack	Jar size	Process Time at Altitudes of		
		0– 1,000 ft	1,001– 6,000 ft	Above 6,000 ft
Hot	Pints	10 min	15	20
	Quarts	15	20	25

Pickled Mixed Vegetables

4 lbs of 4- to 5-inch-long pickling cucumbers, washed, and cut into 1-inch-thick slices (cut off ¹⁄₁₆ of an inch from the blossom end and discard)

2 lbs peeled and quartered small onions

4 cups cut celery (1-inch pieces)

2 cups peeled and cut carrots (½-inch pieces)

2 cups cut sweet red peppers (½-inch pieces)

2 cups cauliflower flowerets

5 cups white vinegar (5%)

¼ cup prepared mustard

½ cup canning or pickling salt

3½ cups sugar

3 tbsp celery seed

2 tbsp mustard seed

½ tsp whole cloves

½ tsp ground turmeric

Yield: About 10 pints

Procedure: Combine vegetables, cover with 2 inches of cubed or crushed ice, and refrigerate 3 to 4 hours. In 8-quart kettle, combine vinegar and mustard and mix well. Add salt, sugar, celery seed, mustard seed, cloves, and turmeric. Bring to a boil. Drain vegetables and add them to the hot pickling solution. Cover and slowly return to a boil. Drain vegetables but save pickling solution. Fill hot, sterile (see page 26) pint or quart jars with vegetables, leaving ½ of an inch of headspace. Add hot pickling solution, leaving ½ of an inch of headspace. Remove air bubbles and adjust headspace if needed. Wipe rims of jars with a dampened, clean paper towel. Adjust lids, and process according to the table at the top of the next page.

Pickled Mixed Vegetables

Recommended process time for Pickled Mixed Vegetables in a boiling-water canner

Style of pack	Jar size	Process Time at Altitudes of		
		0–1,000 ft	1,001–6,000 ft	Above 6,000 ft
Hot	Pints	5 min	10	15
	Quarts	10	15	20

Pickled Bread-and-Butter Zucchini

16 cups fresh zucchini, sliced

4 cups onions, thinly sliced

½ cup canning or pickling salt

4 cups white vinegar (5%)

2 cups sugar

4 tbsp mustard seed

2 tbsp celery seed

2 tsp ground turmeric

Yield: About 8 to 9 pints

Procedure: Cover zucchini and onion slices with 1 inch of water to which the canning salt has been added. Let stand 2 hours, then drain thoroughly. Combine vinegar, sugar, and spices in a Dutch oven or large saucepot, and bring to a boil. Add zucchini and onions, and simmer 5 minutes. Fill hot jars with vegetables and pickling solution, leaving ½ of an inch of headspace. Remove air bubbles and adjust headspace if needed. Wipe rims of jars with a dampened, clean paper towel.

Adjust lids, and process per the table below, or use low-temperature pasteurization as described on pages 83-84.

Pickled Bread-and-Butter Zucchini

Recommended process time for Pickled Bread-and-Butter Zucchini in a boiling-water canner

Style of pack	Jar size	Process Time at Altitudes of		
		0–1,000 ft	1,001–6,000 ft	Above 6,000 ft
Hot	Pints or Quarts	10 min	15	20

Pickled Vegetable Relishes

Chayote and Pear Relish

3½ cups peeled, cubed chayote

3½ cups peeled, cubed Seckel pears

2 cups chopped red bell pepper

2 cups chopped yellow bell pepper

3 cups finely chopped onion

2 serrano peppers, finely chopped

2½ cups cider vinegar (5%)

1½ cups water

1 cup white sugar

2 tsp canning salt

1 tsp ground allspice

1 tsp ground pumpkin pie spice

Yield: About 5 pint jars

Procedure: Caution: Wear plastic or rubber gloves and do not touch your face while handling or cutting hot peppers. If you do not wear gloves, wash hands thoroughly with soap and water before touching your face or eyes. Wash, peel, and cut chayote and pears into ½-inch cubes, discarding cores and seeds. Chop onions and peppers. Combine vinegar, water, sugar, salt, and spices in a Dutch oven or large saucepot. Bring to a boil, stirring to dissolve sugar. Add chopped onions and peppers, and return to a boil. Boil for 2 minutes, stirring occasionally. Add cubed chayote and pears, return to the boiling point, and turn off heat. Fill the hot pint jars with the hot solids, leaving 1 inch of headspace. Cover with boiling cooking liquid, leaving ½ of an inch of headspace. Remove air bubbles and adjust headspace if needed. Wipe rims of jars with a dampened, clean paper towel. Adjust lids, and process.

Chayote and Pear Relish

Recommended process time for Chayote and Pear Relish in a boiling-water canner

Style of pack	Jar size	Process Time at Altitudes of		
		0–1,000 ft	1,001–6,000 ft	Above 6,000 ft
Hot	Pints	15 min	20	25

Piccalilli

6 cups chopped green tomatoes

1½ cups chopped sweet red peppers

1½ cups chopped green peppers

2¼ cups chopped onions

7½ cups chopped cabbage

½ cup canning or pickling salt

3 tbsp whole mixed pickling spice

4½ cups vinegar (5%)

3 cups brown sugar

Yield: About 9 half-pints

Procedure: Wash, chop, and combine vegetables with ½ cup salt. Cover with hot water and let stand 12 hours. Drain, and press vegetables in a clean white cloth to remove all possible liquid. Combine vinegar and brown sugar. Tie spices loosely in a spice bag, add to combination of vinegar and brown sugar in a saucepan, and heat to a boil. Add vegetables and boil gently 30 minutes or until the volume of the mixture is reduced by half. Remove spice bag. Fill hot, sterile jars (see page 26) with hot mixture, leaving ½ of an inch of headspace. Remove air bubbles and adjust headspace if needed. Wipe rims of jars with a dampened, clean paper towel. Adjust lids, and process.

Piccalilli

Recommended process time for Piccalilli in a boiling-water canner

Style of pack	Jar size	Process Time at Altitudes of		
		0–1,000 ft	1,001–6,000 ft	Above 6,000 ft
Hot	Half-pints or Pints	5 min	10	15

Pickle Relish

3 quarts chopped cucumbers

3 cups chopped sweet green peppers

3 cups chopped sweet red peppers

1 cup chopped onions

¾ cup canning or pickling salt

4 cups ice

8 cups water

2 cups sugar

4 tsp of mustard seed

4 tsp turmeric

4 tsp whole allspice

4 tsp whole cloves

6 cups white vinegar (5%)

Yield: About 9 pints

Procedure: Add cucumbers, peppers, onions, salt, and ice to water and let stand 4 hours. Drain and re-cover vegetables with fresh ice water for another hour. Drain again. Combine spices in a spice or cheesecloth bag. Add spices to sugar and vinegar in a saucepan, heat to boiling, and pour mixture over vegetables. Cover and refrigerate 24 hours. Heat mixture to boiling, discard spice bag, and fill hot jars with hot mixture, leaving ½ of an inch of headspace. Remove air bubbles and adjust headspace if needed. Wipe rims of jars with a dampened, clean paper towel. Adjust lids, and process.

Pickle Relish

Recommended process time for Pickle Relish in a boiling-water canner

Style of pack	Jar size	Process Time at Altitudes of		
		0–1,000 ft	1,001–6,000 ft	Above 6,000 ft
Hot	Half-pints or Pints	10 min	15	20

Pickled Corn Relish

16 to 20 medium-size ears (to yield 10 cups fresh, whole-kernel corn) or six 10-ounce packages of frozen corn

2½ cups diced sweet red peppers

2½ cups diced sweet green peppers

2½ cups chopped celery

1¼ cups diced onions

1¾ cups sugar

5 cups vinegar (5%)

2½ tbsp canning or pickling salt

2½ tsp celery seed

2½ tbsp dry mustard

1¼ tsp turmeric

Yield: About 9 pints

Procedure: Boil ears of corn 5 minutes, dip in cold water, and cut whole kernels from cob—or use six 10-ounce packages of frozen corn. Combine peppers, celery, onions, sugar, vinegar, salt, and celery seed in a saucepan. Bring to a boil and simmer

5 minutes, stirring occasionally. Mix mustard and turmeric in ½ cup of the simmered mixture. Add this ½-cup mixture and corn to the remaining hot mixture. Simmer another 5 minutes. If desired, thicken mixture with flour paste (¼ cup flour blended in ¼ cup water) and stir frequently. Fill hot jars with hot mixture, leaving ½ of an inch of headspace. Remove air bubbles and adjust headspace if needed. Wipe rims of jars with a dampened, clean paper towel. Adjust lids, and process.

Pickled Corn Relish
Recommended process time for Pickled Corn Relish in a boiling-water canner

Style of pack	Jar size	Process Time at Altitudes of		
		0–1,000 ft	1,001–6,000 ft	Above 6,000 ft
Hot	Half-pints or Pints	15 min	20	25

Pickled Green-Tomato Relish

10 lbs small, hard, green tomatoes

1½ lbs red bell peppers

1½ lbs green bell peppers

2 lbs onions

½ cup canning or pickling salt

1 quart water

4 cups sugar

1 quart vinegar (5%)

⅓ cup prepared yellow mustard

2 tbsp cornstarch

Yield: About 7 to 9 pints

Procedure: Wash and coarsely grate or finely chop tomatoes, peppers, and onions. Dissolve salt in water and pour over vegetables in large kettle. Heat to boiling and simmer 5 minutes. Drain in colander. Return vegetables to kettle. Add sugar, vinegar, mustard, and cornstarch. Stir to mix. Heat to boiling and simmer 5 minutes. Fill hot, sterile pint jars (see page 26) with hot relish, leaving ½ of an inch of headspace. Remove air bubbles and adjust headspace if needed. Wipe rims of jars with a dampened, clean paper towel. Adjust lids, and process.

Pickled Green-Tomato Relish

Recommended process time for Pickled Green-Tomato Relish in a boiling-water canner

Style of pack	Jar size	Process Time at Altitudes of		
		0–1,000 ft	1,001–6,000 ft	Above 6,000 ft
Hot	Pints	5 min	10	15

Pickled Horseradish Sauce

2 cups (¾ lb) freshly grated horseradish

1 cup white vinegar (5%)

½ tsp canning or pickling salt

¼ tsp powdered ascorbic acid

Yield: About 2 half-pints

Procedure: The pungency of fresh horseradish fades within 1 to 2 months, even when refrigerated. Therefore, make only small quantities at a time. Wash horseradish roots thoroughly, and peel off brown outer skin. The peeled roots may be grated in a food processor or cut into small cubes and put through a food grinder. Combine ingredients and fill sterile jars (see page 26) with the combination, leaving ¼ of an inch of headspace. Seal jars tightly and store in refrigerator.

Pickled Pepper-Onion Relish

6 cups finely chopped onions
3 cups finely chopped sweet red peppers
3 cups finely chopped green peppers
1½ cups sugar
6 cups vinegar (5%), preferably white distilled
2 tbsp canning or pickling salt

Yield: About 9 half-pints

Procedure: Wash and chop vegetables. Combine all ingredients and boil gently until mixture thickens and volume is reduced by half (about 30 minutes). Fill hot, sterile jars (see page 26) with hot relish, leaving ½ of an inch of headspace, and seal tightly. Store in refrigerator and use within one month. **Caution: If extended storage is desired, this product must be processed according to the table at the top of the next page.**

Pickled Pepper-Onion Relish

Recommended process time for Pickled Pepper-Onion Relish in a boiling-water canner

Style of pack	Jar size	Process Time at Altitudes of		
		0–1,000 ft	1,001–6,000 ft	Above 6,000 ft
Hot	Half-pints or Pints	5 min	10	15

Spicy Jicama Relish

9 cups diced jicama (you will need about 4 pounds purchased jicama)

1 tbsp whole mixed pickling spice

1 two-inch-long cinnamon stick

8 cups white vinegar (5%)

4 cups sugar

2 tsp crushed red pepper

4 cups diced yellow bell pepper

4½ cups diced red bell pepper

4 cups chopped onion

2 fresh fingerhot peppers (each about 6 inches long), finely chopped and partially seeded

Yield: About 7 pint jars

Procedure: Caution: Wear plastic or rubber gloves and do not touch your face while handling or cutting hot peppers. If you do not wear gloves, wash hands thoroughly with soap and water before touching your face or eyes.

Wash, peel, and trim jicama; dice. Place pickling spice and cinnamon on a clean, double-layer, 6-inch-square piece of 100 percent cotton cheesecloth. Bring corners together and tie with a clean string. (Or use a purchased muslin spice bag.) In a 4-quart Dutch oven or saucepot, combine spice bag, vinegar, sugar, and crushed red pepper. Bring to a boil, stirring to dissolve sugar. Stir in diced jicama, sweet peppers, onion, and fingerhots. Return mixture to boiling. Reduce heat and simmer, covered, over medium-low heat about 25 minutes. Discard spice bag. Fill hot pint jars with relish, leaving ½ of an inch of headspace. Cover with hot pickling liquid, leaving ½ of an inch of headspace. Remove air bubbles and adjust headspace if needed. Wipe rims of jars with a dampened, clean paper towel. Adjust lids, and process.

Spicy Jicama Relish

Recommended process time for Spicy Jicama Relish in a boiling-water canner

Style of pack	Jar size	Process Time at Altitudes of			
		0–1,000 ft	1,001–3,000 ft	3,001–6,000 ft	Above 6,000 ft
Hot	Pints	20 min	25	30	35

Tangy Tomatillo Relish

12 cups chopped tomatillos

3 cups finely chopped jicama

3 cups chopped onion

6 cups chopped plum-type tomatoes

1½ cups chopped green bell pepper

1½ cups chopped red bell pepper

1½ cups chopped yellow bell pepper
1 cup canning salt
2 quarts water
6 tbsp whole mixed pickling spice
1 tbsp crushed red pepper flakes (optional)
6 cups sugar
6½ cups cider vinegar (5%)

Yield: About 6 or 7 pints

Procedure: Remove husks from tomatillos and wash well. Peel jicama and onion. Wash all vegetables well before trimming and chopping. Place chopped tomatillos, jicama, onion, tomatoes, and bell peppers (all 3 types) in a 4-quart Dutch oven or saucepot. Dissolve canning salt in water. Pour over prepared vegetables. Heat to boiling; simmer 5 minutes. Drain thoroughly through a cheesecloth-lined strainer (until no more water drips through, about 15 to 20 minutes). Place pickling spice and optional red pepper flakes on a clean, double-layer, 6-inch-square piece of 100 percent cotton cheesecloth. Bring corners together and tie with a clean string. (Or use a purchased muslin spice bag.) Mix sugar, vinegar, and the spice bag in a saucepan; bring to a boil. Add drained vegetables. Return to boil; reduce heat and simmer, uncovered, 30 minutes. Remove spice bag. Fill hot pint jars with hot relish mixture, leaving ½ of an inch of headspace. Remove air bubbles and adjust headspace if needed. Wipe rims of jars with a dampened, clean paper towel. Adjust lids, and process according to the table at the top of the next page.

Tangy Tomatillo Relish

Recommended process time for Tangy Tomatillo Relish in a boiling-water canner

Style of pack	Jar size	Process Time at Altitudes of		
		0–1,000 ft	1,001–6,000 ft	Above 6,000 ft
Hot	Pints	15 min	20	25

Pickled Foods for Special Diets

No-Sugar-Added Pickled Beets

7 lbs of 2- to 2½-inch-diameter beets

4 to 6 onions (2- to 2½-inch diameter), if desired

6 cups white vinegar (5%)

1½ tsp canning or pickling salt

2 cups Splenda®

3 cups water

2 cinnamon sticks

12 whole cloves

Yield: About 8 pints

Procedure: Trim off beet tops, leaving 1 inch of stem and roots to prevent bleeding of color. Wash thoroughly. Sort for size. Put similar sizes together, cover with boiling water, and cook until tender (about 25 to 30 minutes). **Caution: Drain and discard liquid.** Cool beets. Trim off roots and stems, and slip off skins. Cut into ¼-inch slices. Peel, wash, and thinly slice onions. Combine vinegar, salt, Splenda®, and 3 cups fresh water in large Dutch oven. Tie cinnamon sticks and cloves in a cheesecloth bag, and add to vinegar mixture. Bring to a boil. Add beets and onions. Simmer 5 minutes. Remove spice bag. Fill hot pint jars with hot beets and onion slices, leaving ½ of an inch of headspace. Cover with boiling vinegar solution, leaving ½ of an inch of headspace. Remove air bubbles and adjust headspace if needed. Wipe rims of jars with a dampened, clean paper towel. Adjust lids, and process.

Variation: *Pickled whole baby beets*—Follow the directions above but use beets that are no more than 1 to 1½ inches in diameter. Pack whole after cooking, trimming, and peeling; do not slice.

No-Sugar-Added Pickled Beets

Recommended process time for No-Sugar-Added Pickled Beets in a boiling-water canner

Style of pack	Jar size	Process Time at Altitudes of			
		0-1,000 ft	1,001-3,000 ft	3,001-6,000 ft	Above 6,000 ft
Hot	Pints	30 min	35	40	45

No-Sugar-Added Sweet Pickle Cucumber Slices

3½ lbs of pickling cucumbers

Boiling water to cover sliced cucumbers

4 cups cider vinegar (5%)

1 cup water

3 cups Splenda®

1 tbsp canning salt

1 tbsp mustard seed

1 tbsp whole allspice

1 tbsp celery seed
4 one-inch-long cinnamon sticks

Yield: About 4 or 5 pint jars

Procedure: Wash cucumbers. Slice ¹⁄₁₆ of an inch off the blossom end and discard. Slice cucumbers into ¼-inch-thick slices. Pour boiling water over the cucumber slices and let stand 5 to 10 minutes. Drain off the hot water, and pour cold water over the cucumbers. Let cold water run continuously over the cucumber slices, or change water frequently, until cucumbers are cooled. Drain slices well. Mix vinegar, 1 cup water, Splenda®, and all spices in a 10-quart Dutch oven or stockpot. Bring to a boil. Add drained cucumber slices carefully to the boiling liquid and return to a boil. Place a cinnamon stick in each empty hot jar, if desired. Fill hot pint jars with hot pickle slices, leaving ½ of an inch of headspace. Cover with boiling pickling brine, leaving ½ of an inch of headspace. Remove air bubbles and adjust headspace if needed. Wipe rims of jars with a dampened, clean paper towel. Adjust lids, and process.

No-Sugar-Added Sweet Pickle Cucumber Slices

Recommended process time for No-Sugar-Added Sweet Pickle Cucumber Slices in a boiling-water canner

Style of pack	Jar size	Process Time at Altitudes of		
		0–1,000 ft	1,001–6,000 ft	Above 6,000 ft
Hot	Pints	10 min	15	20

Reduced-Sodium Sliced Dill Pickles

4 lbs (3- to 5-inch-long) pickling cucumbers

6 cups vinegar (5%)

6 cups sugar

2 tbsp canning or pickling salt

1½ tsp celery seed

1½ tsp mustard seed

2 large onions, thinly sliced

8 heads fresh dill

Yield: About 8 pints

Procedure: Wash cucumbers. Cut ¹⁄₁₆ of an inch off blossom end and discard. Cut cucumbers into ¼-inch slices. Combine vinegar, sugar, salt, celery seeds, and mustard seeds in large saucepan. Bring mixture to boiling. Place 2 slices of onion and ½ head of dill on bottom of each hot pint jar. Fill hot jars with cucumber slices, leaving ½ of an inch of headspace. Top each jar of cucumber slices with 1 slice of onion and ½ head of dill. Pour hot pickling solution over contents of each jar, leaving ½ of an inch of headspace. Remove air bubbles and adjust headspace if needed. Wipe rims of jars with a dampened, clean paper towel. Adjust lids, and process.

Reduced-Sodium Sliced Dill Pickles

Recommended process time for Reduced-Sodium Sliced Dill Pickles in a boiling-water canner

Style of pack	Jar size	Process Time at Altitudes of		
		0–1,000 ft	1,001–6,000 ft	Above 6,000 ft
Raw	Pints	15 min	20	25

Reduced-Sodium Sliced Sweet Pickles

4 lbs (3- to 4-inch-long) pickling cucumbers

Brining solution:	**Canning syrup:**
1 quart distilled white vinegar (5%)	1⅔ cups distilled white vinegar (5%)
1 tbsp canning or pickling salt	3 cups sugar
1 tbsp mustard seed	1 tbsp whole allspice
½ cup sugar	2¼ tsp celery seed

Yield: About 4 to 5 pints

Procedure: Wash cucumbers. Cut ¹⁄₁₆ of an inch off blossom end and discard. Cut cucumbers into ¼-inch slices. Combine all ingredients for canning syrup in a saucepan and bring to a boil. Keep syrup hot until used. In a large kettle, mix the ingredients for the brining solution. Add the cut cucumbers, cover, and simmer until the cucumbers change color from bright to dull green (about 5 to 7 minutes). Drain the cucumber slices. Fill hot jars with cucumber slices, and cover with hot canning syrup, leaving ½ of an inch of headspace. Remove air bubbles and adjust headspace if needed. Wipe rims of jars with a damp-ened, clean paper towel. Adjust lids, and process.

Reduced-Sodium Sliced Sweet Pickles

Recommended process time for Reduced-Sodium Sliced Sweet Pickles in a boiling-water canner

Style of pack	Jar size	Process Time at Altitudes of		
		0–1,000 ft	1,001–6,000 ft	Above 6,000 ft
Hot	Pints	10 min	15	20

Glossary of Terms

Acid foods: Foods that contain enough acid to result in a pH of 4.6 or lower. Includes all fruits except figs; most tomatoes; fermented and pickled vegetables; relishes; and jams, jellies, and marmalades. Acid foods may be processed in boiling water.

Altitude: The vertical elevation of a location above sea level.

Ascorbic acid: The chemical name for vitamin C. Lemon juice contains large quantities of ascorbic acid and is commonly used to prevent browning of peeled, light-colored fruits and vegetables.

Bacteria: A large group of one-celled microorganisms widely distributed in nature. *See* Microorganisms.

Blancher: A 6- to 8-quart, lidded pot designed with a fitted, perforated basket to hold food in boiling water or with a fitted rack to steam foods. Useful for loosening skins on fruits to be peeled or for heating foods to be hot-packed.

Boiling-water canner: A large, standard-size, lidded kettle with a jar rack that is designed for heat-processing 7 quarts or 8 to 9 pints of canned food in boiling water.

Botulism: An illness caused by eating a toxin that is produced by *Clostridium botulinum* bacteria. The bacteria can grow and produce their deadly toxin in moist, low-acid food that contains less than 2 percent oxygen and is stored between 40° and 120°F. Proper heat processing destroys this bacterium in canned food. Freezer temperatures inhibit its growth in frozen food. Low levels of moisture control its growth in dried food. High levels of oxygen control its growth in fresh foods.

Canning: A method of food preservation in which the food is packaged in air-tight, vacuum-sealed containers and heat-processed sufficiently to enable the containers of food to be stored at normal home temperatures.

Canning salt: Regular table salt without the anticaking or iodine additives. *Also called* pickling salt.

Citric acid: A form of acid that can be added to canned foods. It increases the acidity of low-acid foods and may improve the flavor and color.

Cold pack: A canning procedure in which jars are filled with raw food. "Raw pack" is actually the preferred term for describing this practice. "Cold pack" is often used incorrectly to refer to foods that are open-kettle canned or to jars that are heat-processed in boiling water.

Enzymes: Proteins in food that accelerate many flavor, color, texture, and nutritional changes, especially when food is cut, sliced, crushed, bruised, or exposed to air. Proper blanching or hot-packing practices destroy enzymes and improve food quality.

Exhausting: Removal of air from within and around food and from the interior of jars and canners. Blanching exhausts air from live food tissues. Exhausting, or venting, of pressure canners is necessary to prevent a risk of botulism in low-acid canned foods.

Fermentation: Changes in food caused by intentional growth of bacteria, yeast, or mold. Native bacteria ferment (transform) natural sugars to lactic acid, a major flavoring and preservative in sauerkraut and in naturally fermented dills. Alcohol, vinegar, and some dairy products are also fermented foods.

Headspace: The unfilled space above food or liquid in jars. Allows for food expansion as jars are heated and for the formation of vacuums as jars cool.

Heat-processing: Treatment of jars with sufficient heat to enable storing food at normal home temperatures.

Hermetic seal: An absolutely airtight container seal that prevents reentry of air or microorganisms into packaged foods.

Hot pack: The practice of heating raw food in boiling water or steam and filling it hot into jars.

Low-acid foods: Foods that contain very little acid and have a pH above 4.6. The acidity in these foods is insufficient to prevent the growth of *Clostridium botulinum* bacteria. Vegetables, some tomatoes, figs, all meats, fish, seafoods, and some dairy foods are low in acid. To control all risks of botulism, jars of these foods must be (1) heat processed in a pressure canner or (2) acidified to a pH of 4.6 or lower before processing in boiling water.

Microorganisms: Independent organisms of microscopic size, including bacteria, yeast, and mold. When alive in a suitable environment, they grow rapidly and may divide or reproduce every 10 to 30 minutes. Therefore, they reach high populations very quickly. Undesirable microorganisms cause disease and food spoilage. Desirable microorganisms are sometimes intentionally added in order to ferment foods or make antibiotics or for other reasons.

Mold: A fungus-type microorganism. Its growth on food is usually visible and colorful. Molds may grow on many foods, including acid foods such as jams, jellies, and canned fruits. Recommended heat-processing and sealing practices prevent mold from growing on these foods.

Mycotoxins: Toxins produced by the growth of some molds on foods.

Open-kettle canning: A canning method that is NOT recommended. Food is supposedly adequately heat-processed in a covered kettle and then filled hot and sealed into sterile jars. Foods canned this way have low vacuums, or too much air, which permits rapid loss of quality in foods. Moreover, these foods often spoil because they become recontaminated while the jars are being filled.

Pasteurization: The process of heating a specific food sufficiently to destroy the most heat-resistant pathogenic, or

disease-causing, microorganisms that are known to be associated with that particular food.

pH: A measure of acidity or alkalinity. Values range from 0 to 14. A food is neutral when its pH is 7.0. Lower pH values indicate increasingly more acidic food, while foods with pH values higher than 7.0 are increasingly more alkaline.

Pickling: The practice of adding enough vinegar or lemon juice to a low-acid food to lower its pH to 4.6 or less. Properly pickled foods may be safely heat-processed in boiling water.

Pressure canner: A specifically designed metal kettle with a lockable lid used for heat-processing low-acid food. These canners have jar racks, one or more safety devices, systems for exhausting air, and a way to measure or control pressure. Canners with 16- to 23-quart capacity are common. The minimum volume of canner that can safely be used is one that will hold 4 quart jars. Use of pressure saucepans with smaller capacities is not recommended.

Raw pack: The practice of filling jars with raw, unheated food. It is acceptable for canning low-acid foods, but it allows more rapid quality losses in acid foods that are then heat-processed in boiling water.

Spice bag: A closable fabric bag used to infuse pickling solution with spice flavors.

Style of pack: A term referring to the form of canned food, such as whole, sliced, piece, juice, or sauce. The term may also be used to reveal whether food is filled raw or hot into jars.

Vacuum: The state of negative pressure. Reflects how thoroughly air is removed from within a jar of processed food—the higher the vacuum, the less air left in the jar.

Yeasts: A group of microorganisms that reproduce by budding. They are used in fermenting some foods and in leavening breads.

Recipes for Your Extra Garden-Fresh Vegetables

So you've followed the instructions in this guide carefully and put up a year's worth of garden vegetables for your family. Congratulations! You'll be glad, come winter, to be able to serve up flavorful and nutritious vegetable dishes that won't break your budget.

But what if this year's harvest has been even more abundant than usual and, despite canning all you'll need and sharing with neighbors, you still have vegetables on the vine? You certainly don't want to let them go to waste, and there's no need to. Instead, use the spare produce from your garden and the easy recipes in this bonus section to treat your family to some new and creative dishes. You may just find a new family favorite! (Remember, however, that these bonus recipes are not designed to prepare food for canning. These recipes should be made and served fresh.)

Cold Asparagus with Lemon-Mustard Dressing

12 fresh asparagus spears

2 tablespoons fat-free mayonnaise

1 tablespoon sweet brown mustard

1 tablespoon fresh lemon juice

1 teaspoon grated lemon peel, divided

1. Bring ½ cup water to a boil in medium saucepan over high heat. Add asparagus; cook until crisp-tender. Immediately drain and run under cold water. Cover; refrigerate until chilled.

2. Combine mayonnaise, mustard and lemon juice in small bowl; blend well. Stir in ½ teaspoon lemon peel; set aside.

3. Divide asparagus between 2 plates. Spoon 2 tablespoons dressing over top of each serving; sprinkle each with ¼ teaspoon lemon peel. Garnish with carrot strips and edible flowers, such as pansies, violets or nasturtiums, if desired.

Makes 2 appetizer servings

Country Green Beans with Ham

2 teaspoons olive oil

¼ cup minced onion

1 clove garlic, minced

1 pound fresh green beans, rinsed and drained

1 cup chopped fresh tomatoes

6 slices (2 ounces) thinly sliced low-fat smoked turkey-ham

1 tablespoon chopped fresh marjoram
2 teaspoons chopped fresh basil
⅛ teaspoon black pepper
¼ cup herbed croutons

1. Heat oil in medium saucepan over medium heat. Add onion and garlic; cook and stir about 3 minutes or until onion is tender. Reduce heat to low.

2. Add beans, tomatoes, turkey-ham, marjoram, basil and pepper. Cook about 10 minutes, stirring occasionally, until liquid from tomatoes is absorbed. Transfer mixture to serving dish. Top with croutons.

Makes 4 servings

Fresh Limas in Onion Cream

1 pound fresh lima beans
⅔ cup milk
½ teaspoon dried minced onion
1 tablespoon butter or margarine
1 small onion, sliced into rings
⅓ cup sour cream
2 teaspoons sliced pimiento
Salt and black pepper

1. To shell beans, open pods at seams by pinching pods between thumbs and forefingers. Remove beans and discard shells.

2. Place beans in small heavy saucepan. Add milk and minced onion. Bring to a boil over medium heat. Reduce heat to low. Simmer, uncovered, 20 to 25 minutes or until tender.

3. Meanwhile, melt butter in small skillet over medium-high heat. Add onion rings; cook and stir until golden brown. Transfer to lima bean mixture. Stir in sour cream and pimiento. Season to taste with salt and pepper. Transfer to warm serving dish. Garnish as desired. Serve immediately.

Makes 4 side-dish servings

Apricot-Glazed Beets

1 large bunch fresh beets or 1 pound loose beets

1 cup apricot nectar

1 tablespoon cornstarch

2 tablespoons cider vinegar or red wine vinegar

8 dried apricot halves, cut into strips

¼ teaspoon salt

Additional apricot halves (optional)

1. Cut tops off beets, leaving 1 inch of stem. Do not trim root ends. Scrub beets under cold running water with soft vegetable brush, being careful not to break skins.

2. Place beets in medium saucepan; add enough water to cover. Cover saucepan. Bring to a boil over high heat; reduce heat to medium. Simmer about 20 minutes or until skins rub off easily and beets are barely firm when pierced with fork. Transfer to plate; cool. Rinse pan.

3. Combine apricot nectar with cornstarch in same saucepan. Stir in vinegar. Add apricot strips and salt. Cook over medium heat until mixture thickens.

4. Cut roots and stems from beets on plate.* Peel, halve and cut beets into ¼-inch-thick slices. Add beet slices to apricot mixture; toss gently to coat. Transfer to warm serving dish. Garnish as desired. Serve immediately with apricot halves, if desired.
Makes 4 side-dish servings

*Do not cut beets on cutting board, because the juice will stain the board.

Nutmeg & Honey Carrot Crescents
1 pound fresh carrots, cut into ¼-inch crescents
2 tablespoons honey
¼ teaspoon grated nutmeg
2 tablespoons chopped walnuts

1. Place carrots and ⅓ cup water in large saucepan; cover. Bring to a boil over high heat; reduce heat to medium-low. Simmer 8 minutes or until fork-tender.

2. Transfer carrots to warm serving dish. Bring remaining liquid in saucepan to a boil until liquid is almost evaporated. Add honey and nutmeg; stir. Pour over carrots. Toss gently to coat. Sprinkle with walnuts. Garnish as desired. Serve immediately.
Makes 4 side-dish servings

Savory Matchstick Carrots

½ pound carrots, cut into thin strips

1 small turnip,* peeled and cut into thin strips

3 tablespoons butter or margarine, cut into pieces

1½ teaspoons fresh thyme or ½ teaspoon dried thyme leaves

⅛ teaspoon salt

⅛ teaspoon black pepper

*Or, substitute 2 additional carrots for turnip.

1. Place carrot and turnip strips in medium saucepan. Add ½ cup water; cover. Bring to a boil over high heat; reduce heat to medium. Simmer 5 to 8 minutes or until crisp-tender. Drain; set aside.

2. Melt butter over medium heat in same saucepan. Stir in thyme, salt and pepper. Return carrots and turnips to saucepan; toss gently to coat. Transfer carrot mixture to warm serving dish. Garnish as desired. Serve immediately.

Makes 4 side-dish servings

Indian-Style Vegetable Stir-Fry

1 teaspoon vegetable oil

1 teaspoon curry powder

1 teaspoon ground cumin

⅛ teaspoon red pepper flakes

1½ teaspoons finely chopped, seeded jalapeño pepper*

2 cloves garlic, minced

¾ cup chopped red bell pepper

¾ cup thinly sliced carrots

3 cups cauliflower florets

½ teaspoon salt

2 teaspoons finely chopped cilantro (optional)

*Chile peppers can sting and irritate the skin; wear rubber gloves when handling peppers and do not touch eyes. Wash hands after handling chile peppers.

1. Heat oil in large nonstick skillet over medium-high heat. Add curry powder, cumin and red pepper flakes; cook and stir about 30 seconds. Stir in jalapeño and garlic. Add bell pepper and carrots; mix well to coat. Add cauliflower florets; reduce heat to medium.

2. Stir in ¼ cup water; cook and stir until water evaporates. Add an additional ¼ cup water; cover and cook about 8 to 10 minutes or until vegetables are crisp-tender, stirring occasionally.

3. Add salt; mix well. Sprinkle with cilantro, if desired. Serve immediately.

Makes 6 servings

Roasted Corn & Wild Rice Salad

½ cup uncooked wild rice

1½ cups corn (about 3 medium ears)

½ cup diced seeded tomato

½ cup finely chopped yellow or green bell pepper

⅓ cup minced fresh cilantro

2 tablespoons minced seeded jalapeño pepper* (optional)

2 tablespoons fresh lime juice

2 tablespoons honey mustard

1 tablespoon olive oil

½ teaspoon ground cumin

*Chile peppers can sting and irritate the skin; wear rubber gloves when handling and do not touch eyes. Wash hands after handling chile peppers.

1. Bring 1½ cups water to a boil in small saucepan over high heat. Stir in rice; cover. Reduce heat to medium-low. Simmer 40 minutes or until rice is just tender but still firm to the bite. Drain.

2. Preheat oven to 400°F. Coat baking sheet with nonstick cooking spray. Spread corn evenly on prepared baking sheet. Bake 20 to 25 minutes or until corn is lightly browned, stirring after 15 minutes.

3. Combine rice, corn, tomato, bell pepper, cilantro and jalapeño, if desired, in large bowl. Combine lime juice, honey mustard, oil and cumin in small bowl. Drizzle mustard mixture over rice mixture; toss to coat. Cover; refrigerate 2 hours. Serve on lettuce leaves, if desired.

Makes 6 servings

Shrimp Okra Gumbo

¼ cup plus 1 tablespoon vegetable oil, divided

¼ cup all-purpose flour

1 medium onion, chopped

1 small green bell pepper, chopped

2 cloves garlic, minced

1 can (14½ ounces) tomatoes, cut-up and undrained

½ teaspoon dried thyme leaves

½ teaspoon salt

¼ teaspoon ground red pepper

2 bay leaves

8 ounces fresh or frozen okra, cut into ¾-inch slices

1 pound medium raw shrimp, peeled

5 cups hot cooked rice

1. To make roux, cook and stir ¼ cup oil and flour in medium saucepan over medium-low heat 20 minutes or until mixture is tannish-brown color; set aside.

2. Heat remaining 1 tablespoon oil in 5-quart Dutch oven or large saucepan over medium-high heat. Add onion, bell pepper and garlic; cook and stir until vegetables are crisp-tender.

3. Stir in 2½ cups water, tomatoes with liquid, thyme, salt, red pepper and bay leaves. Bring to a boil over high heat. Reduce heat to medium-low; simmer, uncovered, 15 minutes.

4. Stir roux and okra into tomato mixture. Bring to a boil over high heat. Reduce heat to medium-low. Simmer, uncovered, 20 minutes, stirring occasionally.

5. Add shrimp to gumbo and cook 5 minutes or until shrimp turn pink and opaque. Discard bay leaves. Serve gumbo over cooked rice.

Makes 5 servings

Green Pea and Potato Soup

1 can (about 14 ounces) fat-free reduced-sodium chicken broth

1 cup diced peeled potato

1 cup fresh or frozen green peas

½ cup sliced green onion tops

2 leaves green leaf lettuce, chopped

1 teaspoon dried dill weed

⅛ teaspoon ground white pepper

1½ cups buttermilk

Dash paprika

1. Combine broth, potato, peas, green onions, lettuce, dill and pepper in medium saucepan. Bring to a boil over high heat. Reduce heat to medium. Cover; cook 10 minutes or until potatoes are just tender. Let cool, uncovered, to room temperature.

2. Place vegetables and cooking liquid in food processor. Process 45 seconds or until almost smooth. Return mixture to saucepan; stir in buttermilk. Cook and stir over low heat 5 minutes or until heated through. Sprinkle with paprika.

Makes 6 servings

Note: Soup may be served cold. Chill at least 8 hours before serving.

Chicken Chili

1 tablespoon vegetable oil

1 medium onion, chopped

1 medium green bell pepper, seeded and chopped

1 pound ground chicken or turkey

2 fresh jalapeño peppers,* chopped

1 can (28 ounces) tomatoes, cut-up, undrained

1 can (28 ounces) kidney beans, rinsed and drained

1 can (8 ounces) tomato sauce

1 tablespoon chili powder

1 teaspoon salt

1 teaspoon dried oregano leaves

1 teaspoon ground cumin

¼ teaspoon ground red pepper

½ cup (2 ounces) shredded Cheddar cheese

* Chile peppers can sting and irritate the skin; wear rubber gloves when handling and do not touch eyes. Wash hands after handling chile peppers.

1. Heat oil in 5-quart Dutch oven or large saucepan over medium-high heat. Cook onion, bell pepper, and chicken in hot oil until chicken is no longer pink and onion is crisp-tender, stirring frequently to break up chicken.

2. Stir in jalapeño peppers, tomatoes with juice, kidney beans, tomato sauce, chili powder, salt, oregano, cumin and red pepper. Bring to a boil over high heat. Reduce heat to medium-low. Simmer, uncovered, 45 minutes. Spoon hot into bowls, and top with Cheddar cheese.

Makes 6 servings

Roasted Sweet Pepper Tapas

2 medium red bell peppers

1 clove garlic, minced

1 teaspoon chopped fresh oregano or ½ teaspoon dried
   oregano leaves
2 tablespoons olive oil
Garlic bread (optional)

1. Cover broiler pan with foil. Set broiler pan about 4 inches from heat. Preheat broiler. Place peppers on foil. Broil 15 to 20 minutes or until blackened on all sides, turning peppers every 5 minutes with tongs.

2. To peel peppers, place blackened peppers in paper bag. Close bag; set aside to cool about 15 to 20 minutes. Cut around each core, twist and remove. Cut peppers into halves. Place pepper halves on cutting board. Peel off skins with paring knife; rinse under cold water to remove seeds.

3. Lay pepper halves flat and slice lengthwise into ¼-inch strips with chef's knife. Transfer pepper strips to glass jar. Add garlic, oregano and oil. Close lid; shake to blend. Marinate at least 1 hour. Serve on plates with garlic bread, if desired. Or, refrigerate in jar up to 1 week. Garnish as desired.

Makes 6 appetizer servings

Tip: Use this roasting technique for all types of sweet and hot peppers. Broiling time will vary depending on size of pepper. When handling hot peppers, such as Anaheim, jalapeño, poblano or serrano, wear disposable plastic gloves and use caution to prevent irritation of skin or eyes.

Zesty Lentil Stew

1 cup dried lentils

2 cups chopped peeled potatoes

1 can (14½ ounces) fat-free reduced-sodium chicken broth

1½ cups chopped seeded tomatoes

1 can (11½ ounces) no-salt-added spicy vegetable juice cocktail

1 cup chopped onion

½ cup chopped carrot

½ cup chopped celery

2 tablespoons chopped fresh basil or 2 teaspoons dried basil
    leaves

2 tablespoons chopped fresh oregano or 2 teaspoons dried
    oregano leaves

1 to 2 tablespoons finely chopped jalapeño pepper*

¼ teaspoon salt

*Chile peppers can sting and irritate the skin; wear rubber gloves when
handling and do not touch eyes. Wash hands after handling chile peppers.

1. Rinse lentils under cold water; drain. Combine lentils, potatoes, broth, 1⅔ cups water, tomatoes, vegetable juice cocktail,
onion, carrot, celery, basil, oregano, jalapeño pepper and salt in
3-quart saucepan.

2. Bring to a boil over high heat. Reduce heat to medium-low.
Cover; simmer 45 to 50 minutes or until lentils are tender,
stirring occasionally.

Makes 4 servings

Low-Fat Cajun Wedges

Russet potatoes
Nonstick cooking spray
Cajun seasoning or other seasoning, such as paprika

1. Preheat oven to 400°F. Scrub potatoes under running water with soft vegetable brush; rinse. Dry well. Do not peel. Line baking sheet with foil, and spray with nonstick cooking spray.

2. Cut potatoes into halves lengthwise with chef's knife; then cut each half lengthwise into 3 wedges. Place potatoes, skin sides down, in single layer on prepared baking sheet. Spray potatoes lightly with nonstick cooking spray, and sprinkle with seasoning.

3. Bake 25 minutes or until browned and fork-tender. Garnish with purple kale and fresh sage leaves, if desired. Serve immediately.

Makes about 1 serving per potato

Potato Pancakes

1½ pounds russet potatoes, grated
½ cup onion, grated
2 tablespoons chopped chives
¼ teaspoon salt
¼ teaspoon black pepper
½ cup applesauce

1. Combine potatoes, onion, chives, salt and pepper in medium bowl; mix well.

2. Spray large nonstick skillet with nonstick cooking spray. Heat over medium heat until water droplets sprinkled on skillet bounce off surface.

3. Drop potato mixture by ⅓ cupfuls into skillet; flatten with spatula. Cook over medium-high heat 4 to 5 minutes on each side or until pancakes are cooked through. Serve with applesauce.

Makes 6 servings

Microwave Sweet Potato Chips

2 cups thinly sliced sweet potatoes
1 tablespoon packed brown sugar
2 teaspoons margarine

1. Place sweet potatoes, in single layer, in microwavable dish. Sprinkle with water.

2. Microwave at HIGH (100% power) 5 minutes. Stir in brown sugar and margarine; microwave at HIGH 2 to 3 minutes. Let stand a few minutes before serving.

Makes 4 servings

Sweet Potato Bisque

1 pound sweet potatoes, peeled and coarsely chopped
2 teaspoons margarine
½ cup minced onion
1 teaspoon curry powder

½ teaspoon ground coriander
¼ teaspoon salt
⅔ cup unsweetened apple juice
1 cup low-fat buttermilk

1. Bring 2 quarts water and potatoes to a boil in large saucepan over high heat. Cook uncovered 40 minutes or until potatoes are fork-tender. Drain; rinse under cold water until cool enough to handle.

2. Meanwhile, melt margarine in small saucepan over medium heat. Add onion; cook and stir 2 minutes. Stir in curry, coriander and salt; cook and stir about 45 seconds. Remove from heat; stir in apple juice. Set aside until potatoes have cooled.

3. Place potatoes, buttermilk and onion mixture in food processor or blender; process until smooth.

4. Pour soup back into large saucepan; stir in ¼ cup water to thin to desired consistency. (If soup is too thick, add 1 to 2 more tablespoons water.) Cook and stir over medium heat until heated through. Do not boil. Garnish each serving with dollop of plain low-fat yogurt, if desired.
Makes 4 servings

Turkey, Corn and Sweet Potato Soup

1 teaspoon margarine
½ cup chopped onion
1 small jalapeño pepper,* minced

5 cups turkey broth or reduced-sodium chicken bouillon

1½ pounds sweet potatoes, peeled and cut into 1-inch cubes

2 cups cooked turkey, cut into ½-inch cubes

½ teaspoon salt

1½ cups frozen corn

*Chile peppers can sting and irritate the skin; wear rubber gloves when handling and do not touch eyes. Wash hands after handling chile peppers.

1. Melt margarine in 5-quart saucepan over medium-high heat. Add onion and jalapeño pepper; cook and stir 5 minutes or until onion is soft.

2. Add broth, potatoes, turkey and salt; bring to a boil. Reduce heat to low. Cover; simmer 20 to 25 minutes or until potatoes are tender. Stir in corn. Increase heat to medium and cook 5 to 6 minutes. Garnish with cilantro, if desired.

Makes 8 servings

Garden-Vegetable Bulgur Stew

1 tablespoon vegetable oil

1 large onion, chopped

2 medium tomatoes, peeled and chopped

2 medium carrots, peeled and sliced

4 ounces fresh green beans, cut into 1-inch pieces

2 green onions, sliced

¾ cup canned garbanzo beans, drained

1 can (12 ounces) tomato juice (1½ cups)

⅓ cup uncooked bulgur

1 tablespoon dried mint leaves
1 teaspoon dried summer savory leaves
½ teaspoon salt
Dash black pepper
1 small zucchini, sliced

1. Heat oil in 5-quart Dutch oven over medium heat. Add onion; cook and stir until onion is tender.

2. Stir tomatoes, carrots, green beans, green onions, garbanzo beans, tomato juice, 1 cup water, bulgur, mint, savory, salt and pepper into Dutch oven. Bring to a boil over high heat. Reduce heat to medium-low; simmer, uncovered, about 20 minutes or until beans and carrots are slightly tender.

3. Add zucchini to vegetable mixture. Bring to a boil over high heat. Reduce heat to medium-low; simmer, uncovered, about 4 minutes or until zucchini is slightly tender. Serve in bowls and garnish with dollops of sour cream, if desired.
Makes 4 servings